WHAT I WISH I KNEW BACK THEN

Create a Career & Life You Love

CHRISTINA A. SANDOVAL

 FriesenPress

One Printers Way
Altona, MB R0G 0B0
Canada

www.friesenpress.com

ISBN
978-1-03-831987-6 (Hardcover)
978-1-03-831986-9 (Paperback)
978-1-03-831988-3 (eBook)

1. SELF-HELP, PERSONAL GROWTH, SUCCESS

Distributed to the trade by The Ingram Book Company

ENDORSEMENTS AND SUMMARY OF BOOK

What I Wish I Knew Back Then is a must-have resource for any young career professional facing today's world of work. Christina does a brilliant job of taking a holistic approach to career management, focusing on the inside out. Gain inspiration, practical knowledge, and easy-to-implement strategies to help you achieve the success you want. Don't do it alone, let this book help you more confidently navigate your career in these complex times!

—Serena Santillanes, MS, NCC, MCC, LPCC, Founder and President of Career Journeys, Inc.

This is a must-read for career seekers who are starting their journey in the workplace. Regrettably, our society tends to evaluate us primarily on the 10 percent that's outwardly visible, overlooking the 90 percent that comprises our complete selves—our loves, beliefs, hobbies, family, and more. *What I Wish I Knew Back Then* cuts through the fluff, offering readers a tried-and-true roadmap to not only cultivate a compelling personal brand but also navigate their professional career path.

—Bonique Edwards, Transformation Leader | Branding Expert | DEI Trainer

Christina provided me with the tools necessary to hone in on my personal career development, helped me gain recognition of my self-worth, and encouraged me to not settle for anything less than greatness. I can't emphasize enough how valuable her coaching sessions were to me and how they continue to positively impact my personal and career life.

—Sonia Gamino Sand, Educator M.A. Best Practices

The purpose of this book is to help you navigate your career development, whether you are a recent high school grad, a college student, or a young professional just starting off. Each chapter focuses on a specific topic, making it easier to digest and learn about the various factors affecting success. The author offers a guide to finding a career that is the right fit for you, to decision-making and creating goals for your career and life planning. Learn how to create your personal brand as you build your professional portfolio. Become aware of how to overcome common setbacks, such as stress and conflict. Gain insight into how to build confidence, communication skills, effective time management, motivation, meaningful networking, teamwork, and leadership skills and walk away with tips you can immediately apply to the workplace. Life roles and life balance are discussed, pointing out the significance of these in every area of your career path. Mindfulness and inspiring quotes are referenced throughout each chapter to empower you as you plan and move forward in your career journey. The author's personal experiences are shared in funny and heartfelt stories with a piece of wisdom behind each one. This provides a fun and lighthearted way of learning for the reader. Gain these meaningful tips and strategies you don't want to miss as you begin your career and life path.

AUTHOR BIO

Christina A. Sandoval is a career and life coach with a private practice based in Los Angeles, CA. She aspires to see a self-evolution in her clients, that ultimately leads them to thrive in their work and personal lives by being who they truly were meant to be. Her mission is to help people build their life's work and personal legacy that is fulfilling and meaningful to them. Having worked in this field for many years, Christina is a seasoned counselor and instructor in higher education with a master's degree in counseling, a post-graduate certificate in career and life planning, a bachelor's degree in liberal studies, and holds a national credential as a Certified Career Counselor with the National Career Development Association. Christina enjoys traveling and getting to know different cultures in her free time, but her greatest passion is to help people succeed.

Visit christinasandoval.com for more information.

DEDICATION

With much gratitude, this book is dedicated to

Irma E. Diaz and Albert C. Sandoval
my parents, who have always believed in me and helped me believe
in myself

Jeannette A. Sandoval
my sister, for your invaluable insight through this amazing journey
in life

Julian Marshall and Simon James
my kiddos, for your loving support

to all my students and clients
for making me a better counselor and coach

TABLE OF CONTENTS

INTRODUCTION

Welcome to the first steps in your career journey! You made a wise decision in picking up this book. The tips and tricks you learn here will save you a lot of time by helping you to avoid pitfalls during the early stages of your career. Don't get me wrong—trial and error are good lessons for growth, but why not start applying effective tools right away? You'll still go through the journey of learning as you gain real-life experience, but you'll be a step ahead of the game from the outset. If you want to start your path to success now, keep reading.

I would like to share a little about myself, so you know how I arrived here on my journey. Ever since I was a little girl, I wanted to be useful. I would find things to work on so that I could feel proud that I'd accomplished something by the end of the day. My first-ever job was my own business when I was eleven years old. I didn't realize I was starting a business back then. All I knew was that I wanted to do something and feel good about it. I lived in a condo complex where my neighbors paid me to wash their cars. Now, I had some friends in the neighborhood who would get upset because their parents preferred me to clean their cars—I did a better job than their own kids did. This is funny to me now. I wasn't even being competitive; I just wanted to do a good job. I remember using newspaper and Windex to clean the windows perfectly. Yep, I learned some tricks.

During this time, I also started a candy club with the kids in my complex. We would walk to the store down the street to buy all sorts of candy. (I guess you can figure out what I was doing with the money I earned from the car wash business.) We would all hang out in my garage and eat candy: Skittles, Starbursts, Rocky Road bars, everything. I've got the cavities to prove it! Trust me.

I would also put on musical performances with costumes and stage production. I loved being a leader and organizing with the other kids. We invited neighbors out (mostly our parents) to be in our audience. I'd cast who would play Madonna, the backup singers and dancers, and even who would be the person in charge of stage lighting (my little sister held the flashing strobe light, since she was too shy to perform at the time). Clearly it was the 1980's! Those were the days. What I didn't realize was that I was gaining leadership skills. I was learning what it was like to earn my own money, be independent, and implement my own ideas.

I wouldn't seek another job until a few years later when I was sixteen. I did the usual retail and reception jobs for the next few years. I remember when working at a hair and beauty salon, a lady wanted to book a waxing appointment for her face, and I wrote in the appointment book "wax her mustache and beard off." Ha! Did I actually say those words out loud to the client? Goodness, I'm shaking my head in embarrassment right now.

I even worked as a hostess and a food server in a restaurant while going to college. I started gaining experience as a teacher's aide in a preschool, then a teacher's assistant (TA) in an elementary school. I knew I wanted to become a teacher, and I wanted to gain the necessary experience. I taught Phys Ed (PE), and after college I became a kindergarten teacher. I quickly discovered how much I loved coaching the kids with behavioral challenges. As a teacher, you end up spending a lot of time talking to these kiddos on the side, trying to get them in line. Ha! There was one student in my class who was about six years old. Justin had a lot of energy and would sometimes annoy the other children. When speaking to him one-on-one, coaching him to mellow out, I discovered he was quite bright and kind. He was just very intelligent for his age and needed some mental stimulation. Extra attention helped, and he would start to behave better. I loved my students.

After some time, I decided I wanted to use my coaching skills more and work with older students as a counselor. Working as a teacher eventually led me to work with both college students and law school students. I've worked with college students for several years now. The next time I started my own business, it wasn't a car wash but a career and life coaching practice for young professionals.

Today, I enjoy working at the college level as a counselor and instructor, as well as a career and life coach in my private practice. In these pages, I will offer my guidance to help you begin building your future. I will share my own struggles and setbacks and how I overcame them.

This book will help you build the skills needed to succeed as you start your career, including

- Managing your time effectively
- Setting the right goals
- Managing stress in healthy ways
- Being a better learner
- Visualizing the future, you want
- Building your professional network and branding to market yourself
- Practicing your personal and professional skills for success

They say, "You'll find your passion where your pain is." Well, I found my passion in my struggles. I want to help people succeed and thrive in their own career and personal lives. My hope is that you will find this book helpful and meaningful on your own journey.

Each chapter is broken down by topic. You can read them in order if you would like or just read the topics that interest you. Either way, I believe you'll get a lot out of the information shared. I recommend having a journal or notebook handy for writing and activity prompts throughout each chapter.

Let's get started.

CHAPTER 1

Manage Your Time Like a Rock Star

When I was in college, I learned the hard way that time management is key. I missed the memo in high school and didn't develop this skill until college, after some trial and error. I wasted time when I could have completed my goals much faster. If we don't have this essential skill down, it will be difficult to accomplish our goals efficiently, no matter how badly we want to. What do Oprah Winfrey, Bill Gates, and Lebron James have in common? They are all highly successful people for one thing. You have something in common with them too. We all do. We all have only twenty-four hours each day to live our lives and get things done. These highly successful people don't get more hours and therefore have a better chance of getting things done. Instead, they have learned how to manage their time so that they are able to reach their goals and dreams.

What can you do with your twenty-four hours? Yes, it's very important to allow for fun and relaxation time. In fact, it's vital for quality of life and work-life balance, but you must determine your priorities. What are the most important things to you right now? More of your time should be devoted to those things. Consider the following diagram as an example. Write down the most important goal in your life in the biggest box. Then write the second most important in the second biggest box, and so on and so forth. You can even add more boxes if you like. This exercise will put things into perspective for you and give you an idea of how much time you want to spend on each of those goals. The goal in the biggest box is the one you'll spend most of your time on. It helps to have a visual of your short-term and long-term goals.

Some ideas for goals you might have, include school or training, work or job, family commitments, financial goals, personal projects, friends, fun, hobbies, etcetera. These goals may change over time, especially as you complete more and more of them. That's the great thing. You can adjust this based on your needs in the future as well.

SCHEDULING AND STUDY TIME FOR COLLEGE

When you choose your classes each semester, think about how many college units you are committing to. Is it realistic for you? Are you setting yourself up to succeed or to fail? In other words, will you realistically have enough time to devote yourself to the number of classes you're signing up for, or will you only have enough time to work a little in each class? Remind yourself of why you chose to go to college. Think about how you want to give it your all and show your true potential, how you deserve to get the full experience of learning and growing. Barely getting by is not success and won't help you in future classes or in your future profession. Have you heard the phrase "slow and steady wins the race?" Well, it's not a race by any means, but the point is that slow and steady will get you where you want to be with fewer obstacles along the way. Take it little by little, and with each step, you'll get closer to your end goal.

Consider your personal commitments, your work, etcetera. Below is a helpful guide for you when deciding on how many college units to sign up for each academic term. If you are not working while in school, then a full-time class schedule works, usually twelve units in a semester term and six units in a quarter term. If you work full-time or even part-time while going to school, you must strategize your time a bit more.

SUGGESTED SCHOOL AND WORK BALANCE BASED ON A SEMESTER SYSTEM

Work Hours/Week	Number of Units/Semester
0-15 hours	12-15 units
15-20 hours	12 units
20-30 hours	9 units
30-40 hours	6 units
40 or more	3-6 units

In high school, you likely took classes Monday through Friday for the better part of each day—like a full-time job in a sense. Most of your time, you were required to be in class and only a little of your time was required to complete homework assignments and prepare for exams outside of class. In college, it's the opposite. Yes! It is the opposite! We are in class just a few hours a week for each class and most of our time should be set aside for reading, studying, completing assignments, etcetera. If you approach it this way, there are no surprises. You'll already be aware of what the expectations are for successfully completing a college class.

So far, we've discussed a realistic class-unit load based on how many hours you work per week. Next, we will cover the study rule. It is best to devote two study hours per unit you're enrolled in, every week (outside of class). The following is based on a semester. Below is a chart showing how many hours you should be studying per unit load. This is a good way to gauge whether you will be able to handle a certain number of units all at once and if you have enough time to study for the classes.

SUGGESTED STUDY RULE

1 unit	1 hour
3 units	3 hours per week in class
Study rule	2 hours of study per unit per week
6 units (part-time)	6 hours of class time + 12 hours of study = 18 hours per week
12 units (full-time)	12 hours of class time + 24 hours of study = 36 hours per week

The above chart explains the study rule. One unit represents one hour a week in class. Three units represent three hours a week in class. If a student is enrolled in six units, they are in class six hours per week and should set aside double that for studying outside of class (twelve hours per week). This means the student will be in class six hours per week for the six units they're enrolled in, plus they will be studying outside of class for an additional twelve hours per week. The total time this student should devote to school is eighteen hours per week.

If the student decides to do twelve units instead, they will be in class twelve hours per week. They should set aside study time for twenty-four hours per week. The total time devoted to this full-time schedule should be thirty-six hours per week. This is a good way to make sure you're putting in enough time for as many classes as you choose to take in a semester. Here you can see that a full-time school schedule is like a full-time job (36 hours per week). It would be difficult to manage this if you're already working full-time. Imagine having to squeeze in two full-time jobs!

What does study time include exactly? Study time includes reviewing your class notes, completing reading and homework assignments, creating a study guide, and preparing for an upcoming exam or class project (see Chapter 4 for study tips). This study-time effort is what will help you do well in your classes.

WORKPLACE WEEKLY GOALS AND TO-DO LISTS

How you spend your time during a regular workday is important. You're spending about six to eight hours in one day working on tasks and projects. Reflect on your goals for the week and how you will work toward those goals every day with baby steps. Write down each goal and what you plan to complete for that week. Then create a to-do list. The list will help you stay on task and manage your time efficiently throughout each day. It feels great to check off each item on the list as you complete them. You can even break it down as a to-do list for each day if that works for you. Each item on your to-do list should be brief. You can reflect on the greater details as you start to work on them. The list and any notes you take will serve as a good reminder throughout the day. Another benefit is that you can keep track of your progress every day. It feels good to look back on your workday and know you got a lot done and were productive. This is a rewarding feeling and will pay off greatly when you and your colleagues see how much you're contributing in a timely manner. You start to meet your goals and maybe even exceed your goals with practice. Success doesn't just happen. It comes from forming good habits, like this, along the way; habits that lead you to where you want to be.

> "Success isn't always about greatness. It's about consistency. Consistent hard work leads to success. Greatness will come" (Brookz, 2019).
>
> —Dwayne "The Rock" Johnson, actor, businessman, and professional wrestler

When creating a to-do list or deciding what order you will take on your tasks, consider the level of urgency or deadlines for each item. Obviously, you would tackle the ones that are due earliest. But when you have a few that have similar deadlines or can be done in no particular order, how do you strategize your approach? I find it helpful to tackle the toughest ones first, the ones that will require the most time and effort. Work at one at a time so you maintain your mental focus and devote a hundred percent of your effort. Then work on smaller, easier tasks next. Bigger tasks may be more stressful if you have less time to do them later. That's why I tackle those first, so if anything goes wrong or I have a setback, at least I have most of the day ahead of me to fix it. Find what works for you. This is also a good way to avoid procrastination. Procrastination is something I know many college students and young professionals struggle with. Putting off important work until the last minute will no doubt cause stress we don't need. Stress affects our productivity and the quality of work we put out there. And most importantly, it can negatively affect our health. More about managing stress in Chapter 3.

When I work on planning an event or project, I create a checklist and/or a to-do list. I will then work on each task little by little, step by step. This way, I don't get overwhelmed trying to complete everything at the same time or at the last minute. Again, baby steps will make it smooth and manageable. By the time the deadline comes, you have it all done and even have time and room to adjust and make improvements, resulting in your best work. Whether it's school or training or work, always try to put your best foot forward. Trust me, your effort will eventually bear fruit.

Something I struggled with in the past is perfectionism. Being a perfectionist can get in the way. I had an issue with getting things done. I discovered it was because I wanted things to be perfect, so I would have a hard time making it through all the steps to completion. I got stuck on one step and couldn't move on until things were perfect. Well? I had to remind myself, over and over, life is not perfect. We humans are not perfect. And if we want to succeed, we must be willing to make mistakes and fail from time to time. Failure is a step toward success because we learn from our failures. Without them, we wouldn't learn and grow toward improvement and success. All you must do is try your best. That's it! It will pay off. Trust me, my friend. I would not lead you astray.

Another way to tackle this is to set a time limit for each task. For example, you might give yourself an hour on something and commit to taking a break after that hour is up. Another example is giving yourself a week to complete a project or assignment. This will help in making sure you break up your time efficiently, but you also give yourself a deadline and stick to it. I hope you find that these small tips make a big difference in your productivity.

YOUR CALENDAR IS YOUR GUIDE

Another important time management tool is a calendar. You can use a paper calendar, but I find an electronic calendar to be the best. Apple and Google, to name two, are free and you can use the calendar on your computer and smart phone. There are other apps too. This is convenient when you are on the go! Just pull out your phone and view or edit your calendar when needed. If you're not used to using a calendar, here is a list of ideas for what to include on your own personal calendar:

- Work-shift times
- Class/training times
- Study times spread out throughout each week
- Physical activity (important for health and balance)
- Personal/family commitments
- Important work or school deadlines
- Assignment due dates
- Meeting times
- Recreational/relaxation times/events (this is important for balance in your life)
- Hobby/self-reflection

Get the picture? Whatever you include on your calendar, you will most likely complete it. You are making it a priority in your life and making it clear to your unconscious mind that this is important to you. If it's not on my calendar, I will surely forget all about it.

Now, you may have a separate work calendar that is used for your team and scheduling meetings, etcetera. But I find it most helpful to focus on one calendar as your main life calendar, so you are merging the two together in a simple and brief manner. The role you step into at work or school is different than the role you have in your personal life. Merging the two on one calendar keeps them both a priority and helps you to focus on the two roles in your life that are valuable to you. Sure, you can turn off work mode when you're not working, but keep your awareness and focus in tune with that role.

If you ever have trouble deciding what to prioritize or feel overwhelmed with all the things you must get done, ask yourself this: If you are saying yes to one thing, what are you saying no to (projects, people, patterns)? Remember, we only have twenty-four hours a day to take steps toward our goals. You're not in a hurry, but you should devote quality time and effort to the things that are important to you.

You deserve that my friend. I make my calendar a priority every single day. You can even include tasks you want to complete each day on your calendar and check them off as you complete each one. This is helpful if you're like me, forgetful about details.

I like to use all the different features of a calendar: the at-a-glance monthly view, the weekly view, and the single day view. The at-a-glance allows you to see the main events or items in one month, for example. The day and weekly views allow you to see more detail, such as tasks and to-dos. Color coding helps to organize the information. For example, I have all my monthly bills in green, and I change them to yellow as I pay them off. I have my work-related items all in one color, and my personal items all in another color. This sounds like a lot of work, but once you have a system down, it is less work for yourself to stay organized. I also find the notifications in an electronic calendar to be good reminders. I set mine to thirty minutes before the next appointment, meeting or event. You can modify your calendar however works for you, based on what you enjoy and find useful. That's the beauty of it—being able to create it and make it your own. I'll tell you one thing: I'm rarely late or unprepared for anything. Thanks to my calendar.

MORE TIME MANAGEMENT TIPS

Consistency is key. Getting into a routine that you stick to will aid in forming good habits. A regular routine is consistent. This consistency will lead you to your goal but also allow for flexibility when your agenda needs to be adjusted. Give yourself space and time to reflect and make changes. With each thing you do, be present in that moment. Block out distractions so you can focus your mind on the task at hand. Reward yourself when you complete a task, a weekly goal, or a milestone in your journey. Take a moment to reflect on your hard work and acknowledge that you kept at it, instead of giving up. Be aware that there will be times you need to say no to doing something that doesn't fit in with your plan. This can be a no to yourself when you feel like doing one thing, but you know you should do something else instead. This can also be a no to an invite or to someone who wants or needs something from you. The idea is to organize those things in your life that are important to you by creating boundaries for yourself and others. This is a form of respect for you and your goals. Everyone has their own set of goals and unique journey in life, so people will understand and respect your wishes (generally speaking).

Collaboration

The ability to collaborate is part of a successful path. When things get tough, there is nothing wrong with asking for help, whether in school or in the workplace. You might be working on a group assignment at school or on a team project at work and need to delegate or share some tasks with others. It is completely acceptable to collaborate with others to get things done well and in a timely manner. Oftentimes, two heads are better than one. And this can reduce stress and anxiety around a project.

I remember when I was younger, when my grandma was still alive, she would say "cada cabeza es un mundo." The literal translation is every head (mind) is a world (of its own). Meaning, every person's mind is its own whole world of thoughts, experiences and ideas. Imagine when you bring multiple people to the table, coming from diverse experiences and talents! Magic can happen. Team up, connect and build with others. Helping each other can really foster an environment of growth and development in your area of expertise my friend. Plus! Think of how much more productive you can be in less time.

Timewasters

Now, think about how you spend your time each day. What are some of your timewasters? Below are a few ideas:

- Social media scrolling
- Emails
- Unexpected visitors
- TV watching
- Non-urgent distractions from family/friends

How can you limit your time spent on your timewasters? One example is limiting your social media and TV intake to an hour a day. If we don't pay attention to how much time we are doing these things, quite a bit of time can go by very fast without us being aware of it. Remember, we all have only twenty-four hours in a day.

Multi-tasking is another thing that can take us off track. Sure, in some cases it's great to be able to multi-task. But in most cases, it makes it harder to focus and makes things overwhelming. Studies have shown we actually lose time switching back and forth between tasks and can lose productivity. Clear your area of distractions and try your best to focus on one task at a time.

Health

Making time to stay healthy is also important in time management, because our physical health helps us have the energy to get important things done. Likewise, mental wellness helps us to stay focused and motivated. Emotional wellbeing gives us a healthy mindset and can be achieved in various ways. I suggest regular physical activity, a nutritious diet, reading, leisure, and recreation. Do things you enjoy. This is very important. Stay on top of your mental and physical health by seeing a doctor once a year. Discuss any issues. This way you are being proactive and preventative when it comes to a healthy lifestyle. You can learn how to manage stress in Chapter 3.

One way to avoid stressful situations is to spread out your tasks in a timely manner so you're not stuck cramming everything at the last minute. I try to avoid procrastination by scheduling what I want to get done on my calendar and by sticking to the timeline I set for myself.

Ever feel drained and exhausted from working so hard? What can you do to feel better physically and mentally? Perhaps a hike in nature or a massage? This will help you rest and reconnect with your purpose. You will feel rejuvenated and can come back to working on your goals with good energy and clear focus. Find what works for you. Every bit of self-care makes a difference in how we can manage our time effectively. All your efforts are all interconnected and affect one another.

To recap:

- Establish a routine but be flexible by allowing for adjustments.
- Block out distractions when studying or working.
- Reward yourself when you have completed something.
- Find support/resources to help you.
- It's okay to say no.
- Limit timewasters.
- Avoid multi-tasking.
- Maintain self-care for your mind, body, and soul.
- Avoid procrastination.

In this chapter, we discussed how we can improve our time management by scheduling and managing school and work together, setting weekly work goals, following to-do lists, using a calendar, collaborating with others, avoiding timewasters, and improving our self-care.

The next important part of time management is setting bigger life goals. Which brings us to the next chapter. How can you come up with a goal and create an efficient plan to make it happen? Let's jump in!

CHAPTER 2
Start with Goal Setting

Want to set your life goals, so you know where you're going and what you're working towards? Setting an important goal requires deciding to do so in the first place (more on decision-making later in this chapter). Studies show that setting a goal early on in your college or career journey increases the likelihood that you will complete your educational and career goals. It's difficult to work hard toward something when we don't even know what it is. We don't want to work aimlessly. We won't feel very motivated to do so. Think of your goal as your guiding light, the bright star in the dark sky above, showing you the way. The decisions you make, big or small, should align with your goals in life. If the decision to do one thing interferes with your goal, you know it's probably not the best decision.

Have you heard of the fancy word "congruency"? If all aspects of your life align with your goals, they are congruent with one another. You will have a smoother and more peaceful journey because all the things you do support each other. For example, maybe you choose to go to one party over the weekend instead of two so you can have enough time to study for the big test on Monday. That decision supports your goals. Another example is deciding to volunteer to work on a project at your job, so it helps you learn to do something new.

That new skill may help you in your future job search or promotion at work. Every choice we make affects us in some way, big or small.

What are your top three goals in going to college or vocational school? Write these down for reference. Another way to think about it is: What do you want to get out of college or vocational school? Don't stop at the degree or certification completion. Think about what else you are gaining from getting this education or training, in the present and in the future. Think as big as you want.

HOW TO CREATE EFFECTIVE GOALS FOR YOURSELF

Have you heard of a SMART goal? This is an acronym for

> **S**pecific
>
> **M**easurable
>
> **A**chievable
>
> **R**elevant
>
> **T**ime-based
>
> (Doran, Cunningham, Miller 1981, 35-36)

Example: Goal = complete my education

S—Be specific. What educational goal exactly? What area of study or major? Will you earn a two-year degree or four-year degree? Certificate?

M—What are the measurable steps? Lay out in detail each step you'll take to complete the goal, so it is measurable, and you know that you are taking steps toward it.

A—Is it achievable and realistic? Think about your commitments and responsibilities. With this in mind, is this goal feasible? Is it doable? Will you have the time and energy to do it? Do you want to invest yourself in this?

R—Is this goal relevant for you? How will this goal help your future? Why do you want this goal? What does it mean to you?

T—What is the time frame for completing the goal? How long will you give yourself to complete it? Two years, four years, six months?

Sit down and write down the answers to each question above. You'll know if your goal meets the SMART criteria for a goal that aligns with your life. Be flexible. As you start to take each step toward achieving your goal, be sure to not only reward yourself when completing small steps, but also assess your progress. If it is not working well, be willing to adjust your plan as needed. Make it happen.

> "Setting goals is the first step in turning the invisible into the visible" (Collection, 2022).
>
> —Tony Robbins, author and motivational speaker

HOW TO MAKE THOSE BIG DECISIONS

It's easier to make a smaller decision than a bigger one. This is because the bigger the decision, the greater the impact it has on your life. This process can be stressful and overwhelming. Remind yourself that all of us need to face failures from time to time to achieve the success we desire. So don't be afraid of making mistakes. Again, I always go back to the following: Just try your best in everything you do. That's all any of us can ever do. It will eventually come together the way it's supposed to be for us. We need to trust that. Life is all about exploring and learning. Enjoy the process! Think of it this way: The decisions we make today will lead to more choices later.

Let me give you an example. When I was a college student years ago, I thought I knew what I wanted to do for work for my entire life. I was convinced I wanted to be an elementary school teacher forever. I went to school and trained for this career. Every job I took after making this decision aligned with this goal, and it was meant to help me gain experience toward that goal. I started working as a teacher's assistant with different age groups. Then I started getting substitute teaching positions. Well, I eventually reached my end goal to become a lead teacher for elementary grades. I was a teacher for a few years. But that beautiful dream led me to discover my passion for counseling and coaching and helping others succeed in a lot of different ways, not just teaching subjects in school. I don't know if I would have found this passion if it wasn't for the original goal of being a teacher. Therefore, my decision to be a teacher so long ago was the right one for a season in my life that eventually led me to another goal/season in my career. Plus, the experience was invaluable and has helped me in other types of jobs I've had.

I like to imagine a puzzle, where all the pieces of your life are put together and make you who you are today. All your life experiences make the puzzle pieces that will eventually come together and form a beautiful picture or journey that is only yours, no one else's. You are unique in all your experiences and strengths like a mosaic of different colors, shapes, and sizes of pieces that, when placed side by side, shine ever so brightly.

I want to share with you some suggestions for a solid checklist when making decisions, especially life-altering ones. I came across this checklist while training at one of the schools I worked for. The presenter gave this to us as a resource for our students as we guided their career choices. It's a "Decision Checklist" (Career Journeys, 2016).

Decision Checklist:

Item	Notes
Check in with both sides of your brain.	Find the balance between emotion and reason. It's important to factor in both logic and how you feel about it.
Visualize your future successful self.	When you have a positive mental image of your success, you begin to believe you can make it. You must believe before you can achieve.
Recognize the power behind each decision you make.	Understand the effects of your decision. Any decision you make causes a chain of events to happen.
Go with your gut.	When you find yourself wavering between two options, your intuition is one of your most powerful decision-making tools.
Don't ask people what you should do.	Having too many outside opinions can cause you to second-guess yourself. However, feel free to consult with the people who will be directly affected by your decision.
Ask yourself the right questions.	What do I want in this lifetime? Will the outcome of my decision move me closer to what I truly want? Does the benefit outweigh the cost? Is the level of risk worth the reward? How committed am I to this change?
Align your life with your core values.	Make your decisions based on whether or not they align with your highest values, passions, and priorities, or it's not going to feel like you made the right choice.
Whatever you decide to do, have grit and gusto!	Make sure you're doing something that motivates you to persevere (despite failure). There's power in your passion.

(CAREER JOURNEYS, 2016)

If you can go through the above checklist and feel good about each response regarding your goal, you can be confident in making a decision that is best for you. We all need a little guidance from time to time. Take advantage of this little tool. It is helpful. If your goal doesn't pass this test, you can make some adjustments to your plan until it feels right.

After you've done your research and considered the pros and cons of a decision, look at it from all angles and see how you feel about the decision you're leaning toward. Maybe this checklist will serve you well when choosing a major in college or when choosing a career or changing jobs (more in Chapter 5). I want you to feel good and confident about important decisions in your life. A commitment can be overwhelming if your heart is not in it. If you deeply care about it and are excited about it, you will be fully committed.

When it comes to our thoughts, we can talk our way in or out of anything. However, at the end of the day you need to feel peace about your decisions. This is when your emotions are a helpful guide. This is your intuition, your inner voice, which knows what's best for you. Be aware that our mind will tell us all kinds of things, but our body will never lie. What are you feeling? Is there tension or pain anywhere in your body? What feelings are you experiencing? Fear, happiness, peace? Make note of these. We must pay attention to what our body is telling us. If our body is relaxed and calm (no tension or pain), we know it's telling us that this is good for us. If we are tense from worrying and maybe even have an unsettling stomach, then we know it's probably not good for us. If I ever feel very nervous about something, I reconsider and evaluate it thoroughly before moving forward. Little nerves are okay and normal but just be aware.

If you are in the middle of making any big decision right now, stop and ask yourself the above questions. You can write down your answers or just acknowledge them in your mind.

Take a deep breath and ponder your responses and awareness.

"Once you make a decision, the universe conspires to make it happen" (Bolton, 2019).

—Ralph Waldo Emerson, essayist, lecturer, philosopher, abolitionist, and poet

As you pursue your goals and take the next steps, pause and reflect from time to time. Remind yourself of why you made this goal. How will this goal change your life for the better? What is its purpose? Keep your eye on the prize and always move forward with that original intention!

What is a big goal you have right now? Write this down. Writing it down is very powerful. You've put your thoughts and desires down on paper. That is the beginning of creating something new. Write down your goal. Then write down how this goal meets the SMART goal criteria. Congratulations! You have set a goal. Now create an action plan to make this goal happen.

YOUR ACTION PLAN

List specific steps you'll take. Include timeline, resources, barriers (if any), and desired results for each step below.

State your goal_____.

Action steps	Timeline	Resources	Potential Barriers	Desired Results

Action steps	Timeline	Resources	Potential Barriers	Desired Results

How will you reward yourself when you've completed each step above?

You can use the time management tips you learned in the previous chapter to manage your goals and plan for each step. As you think of the steps needed for any goal, you might feel adrenaline or a sense of urgency. This is normal. We might start to feel stressed if there's too much to manage. That's why it's important to organize your time and take baby steps (more tips in Chapter 1). Small and steady steps toward your goals make it more manageable.

Keep in mind, sometimes we need stress in our lives. That's right. It's true. Do you want to know what good stress versus bad stress is? Read on.

CHAPTER 3

Manage Stress so It Works for You

My first time serving a table at a restaurant . . . I was so nervous!

When I was eighteen years old, I was a restaurant hostess and would beg my manager to let me wait on tables so I could make tips. He said, "Once you can balance out your cash register, you can start to wait on tables." Ouch! Okay, so I was always off a few cents.

One day, he let me take my very first table. It was four people in business suits, one lady and three men. They seemed so serious and intimidated by the man who appeared to be their boss. He seemed very confident and arrogant in his demeanor and the way he spoke. I brought them four cups of coffee as they requested. A minute later, the boss guy called me over and said, "Can you stick your finger in my coffee and stir it for me?"

Back then, I was a bit naïve and took things literally. Yep, I had a dumb moment and went ahead and stuck my finger in his coffee; I thought it might be cold and that was his way of letting me know. When I felt it was still hot, I quickly realized, *Uh oh, I'm in trouble.*

Even though this was his sarcastic and rude way of asking for a spoon, everyone busted up laughing at that moment. They couldn't believe I'd done it! It made for some good entertainment, apparently. I think they thought I was sticking it to him for being sarcastic. I was mortified, but looking back now, it's funny.

21

In the same restaurant, I finally became an official food server and started making more money on tips. The owners of the restaurant would come in from time to time to see how things were running and would have a meal themselves. One day, the matriarch of the family-owned business was visiting and enjoying her lunch when I had a mishap. It was a busy rush hour with lots of tables full of people. I was carrying a large tray full of warm plates out to a table when, oops, I tripped and dropped the whole thing on the floor. Down came all the plates, breaking on the ground, food everywhere. This happened right in front of the owner. I was so embarrassed and thought, *Oh, no! She's gonna think I'm a horrible waitress! Eek!* Of course I cleaned up the mess right away.

Luckily, she didn't say anything and didn't make a big deal out of it. I felt bad for the people who had to wait for their food to be cooked again.

A year or two later, when I got the hang of being a food server, I started working for a more upscale restaurant affiliated with a hotel. We would facilitate banquet events and fancy dinners in the dining area. I was still having a hard time opening wine bottles—I always got cork floaties in the wine—but was doing pretty well overall! One night, I brought over a small tray of drinks for a table. Again, I tripped and ended up spilling the tray of drinks on one of the gentlemen at the table. His suit was soaked. *Eek!* Not so fancy of me.

I wanted to share with you these funny, embarrassing moments I've had so you can see that everyone makes mistakes and can find themselves in stressful situations at times, but we can recover and still do well. You'll notice, despite my mishaps, I was still able to progress from a first-time food server to officially a food server and then a fancy food server. I must have been doing something right! I was getting better with each error. Also, I think attitude and personality go a long way. I remember getting exhausted from working on my feet for hours day after day, but I was grateful I could make my own money so I could buy a car and pay my college expenses. I also had fun with the social aspect of working in a restaurant and met a lot of nice people. There were bummer moments of stress, but I kept my head up and kept moving forward. I knew these moments were just stepping-stones, and I wouldn't be stuck doing this forever. Your mindset makes a huge impact on your everyday life but also on your progress and the opportunities it will attract for you.

WHAT DOES STRESS LOOK LIKE AND FEEL LIKE?

What is stress exactly? We must understand what it is before we can properly manage it. Stress alters your natural balance. It is the body's reaction to harmful situations, whether they are real or perceived. This includes mental, emotional, or physical harm. The following are some signs of stress:

- Fight or flight response
- Increased heart rate
- Quickened breathing
- Tight muscles
- Blood pressure rises

A typical amount of low stress can easily be dealt with and over-come, but severe stress can lead to depression or other serious health conditions over time. Nearly 40 percent of college students experience depression that impacts their performance. More than a thousand suicides occur on college campuses each year across the U.S. There are tools at our fingertips to help us cope with stress in healthier ways. Stress is a normal part of being human, so what can we do about it?

First, determine whether it is good stress or bad stress. Good stress helps us accomplish our goals. It gives us the adrenaline we need to get things done or to protect ourselves from harm. Good stress can give us energy and the drive that we need. Bad stress, on the other hand, can make us feel overwhelmed, fearful, depressed, anxious, and can even bring on physical illness. When we experience bad stress, it can affect all aspects of our lives—our emotions, behavior, thinking ability, and physical health. So here you see that this can really get in the way of other things you want to do—your personal goals and enjoying your life.

What causes bad stress? Some stressors can be due to deadlines at work or school, unpreparedness, obstacles, arguments, danger, or financial hardship, just to name a few.

Stress symptoms to look out for:

- Headache
- Loss of sleep
- Fatigue
- Foggy mind
- Acne
- Frequent sickness
- Decreased energy

The above symptoms may be caused by stressors like the following:

- Not having enough time to do everything
- Procrastination
- Being overworked
- Financial problems
- Family hardships
- Illness

HOW DO WE COPE WITH STRESS IN HEALTHY WAYS?

First, know what not to do. Some people cope with stress in more negative and unhealthy ways without realizing it. This includes alcohol consumption, denial, drug use, overeating, fault-finding, overindulging, or acting out in anger.

Healthy and positive ways to cope with stress are things like being flexible, setting limits, keeping faith, conflict resolution, laughter, relaxation, and deep breathing.

The American Psychological Association (APA) gives the following simple tips to help manage stress (Anton 2015, 5):

1. Identify what is causing the stress and take a break from the stressor.
2. Eat nourishing food and exercise regularly.
3. Do activities you enjoy, smile, and laugh.
4. Get social support from family, friends and counseling.
5. Rest your mind, with meditation and relaxation exercises.
6. Avoid drugs and alcohol.
7. Stay focused on the positive and avoid negative energy.

More In-depth Tips:

- Practice good time management by prioritizing your tasks (more in Chapter 1).
- Set SMART goals (more in Chapter 2). You can redefine your goals and set sensible standards. Be realistic. Do not try to achieve the impossible.
- Avoid procrastination.
- Practice good sleep habits. Go to bed at the same time every night and get six to eight hours of sleep.
- Start a journal. Write down your feelings.
- Plan leisurely activities that help you relax (sports, yoga, massage, meditation, prayer, reading, etcetera).
- Enjoy life and have fun (socializing, hobbies, creativity, fun activities, etcetera).
- Distract yourself. For a problem that can't be resolved right away, take a break from worrying about it. Go out with a friend. Maybe see a movie. It can be a nice, healthy escape.

- Repeat affirmations (more about this in Chapter 7).
- Clear your mind using deep breaths and organize your space and environment.
- Learn conflict resolution skills (more on this in Chapter 7).
- Seek professional help from a doctor or therapist.
- Keep the faith. Believe that things will get better with time and effort.

MINDFULNESS

Controlling your mind, so it doesn't control you, is key. This means we must be aware of our thoughts. Allow them to come and go. It's okay when a bad thought comes in. Just be sure to acknowledge it to yourself and how it makes you feel. Then let it go. You are not your thoughts! They are just visitors passing by. Same thing with your emotions and feelings. These are normal human experiences, whether good or not so good. Don't try to suppress these and push them out. Instead, stop what you're doing and be in the moment. Acknowledge how you're feeling. Give yourself permission to feel that way and accept that it is what you are feeling in that moment because you are human.

Once you've sat with that feeling for a bit, you can let it go. Breathe it in and then breathe it out. Try not to identify with your thoughts and feelings. They come and go. You are just observing them. You're not becoming them. This practice of observation helps to bring you to the present moment, to stop dwelling on the past or worrying about the future. Are you okay in this present moment? If yes, great! Be present in this moment. Oftentimes, we worry about what could go wrong instead of focusing on what is good right now.

"Peace is the result of retraining your mind to process life as it is, rather than as you think it should be" (and Love, 2020).

—Dr. Wayne W. Dyer, self-help author and motivational speaker

I used to suffer from severe anxiety. This could have been caused by stress or a traumatic experience. Either way, I remember having anxiety and panic attacks that were debilitating. I was desperate to do something about it and free myself from this awful feeling. I increased my yoga practice and hiked with friends more often because physical activity helps. I was more aware of what I was eating and if it had any nutritional value (because this affects how you feel), so I improved my diet. Meditation helped to calm my mind. I started doing more of what I love, spending time with family and friends, reading and listening to music. I spoke to a therapist for support and learned about coping tools I could use on my own.

One book that changed my life, *The Power of Now* by Eckhart Tolle, is where I learned how to keep my mind at peace. Being present in the moment is healing. Being present means your mind is in the present. Be aware of your thoughts and observe them, rather than identifying with them. Again, you are not your thoughts (Tolle 2004). We must train ourselves not to dwell on the past and not to worry about the future. But what I found is that it's easy once you become more aware of what is going on in your mind. It becomes second nature.

I realized that it takes many factors, not just one thing, to make a real change for improvement. I encourage you to do the same. Find what works for you, something that is healing and enjoyable. By the way, happiness and laughter are real stress busters. Go get them!

In your journal or notebook, list three to five things that cause you stress. Your awareness of these will help you start to cope with them in healthy ways, as discussed above. Think about how you will consciously cope when these stressors come up. Be aware that even if you don't experience a lot of stress right now, you can develop a healthy lifestyle that will prevent chronic stress in the future. We can put these tips to use in our personal lives and our work lives, creating balance. Not only does this make us happier and more at peace, but it also helps us to focus better and do a better job at being a human (friend, co-worker, leader).

Checking in: In the last few chapters you have learned about effective time management tools, setting SMART goals, and coping with stress in healthy ways. All of the topics in this book are interconnected and affect each other in some way. This is really about becoming a self-aware and grounded person as you pursue your personal and professional endeavors. In the next chapter, you will continue to build your self-awareness and learn many ways in which you can further develop into the person you want to be.

CHAPTER 4

Self-Development Is Key, People

YOUR LEARNING STYLE

Discover how you learn best so that when you are presented with new information, you can easily take it in and understand it in a way that best suits you. Below is a list of the different learning styles, as outlined in Gardner's Theory of Multiple Intelligences (Gardner 1983). A person can have one style they tend to be comfortable with the most but may also have a mix of a few.

Visual Learners: Graphs, pictures, diagrams, flash cards, demonstrations
Auditory Learners: Lecture, music, dialogue
Physical Learners: Learning by doing
Verbal Learners: Discussion and reiterating in your own words
Logical Learners: Taking in facts and statistics
Social Learners: Interaction with others and group learning
Solitary Learners: Learning and working alone
Naturalistic (added in 1995): Relates parts of a grander ecosystem

WIKIPEDIA: HTTPS://EN.WIKIPEDIA.ORG/WIKI/
THEORY_OF_MULTIPLE_INTELLIGENCES

Instructors, trainers, and leaders usually teach based on their own learning style, but good teachers will give opportunities for all students to learn with different learning styles, as they understand that everyone learns differently. If you find yourself in a situation where one style is being used but it doesn't work for you, create ways to learn the information in your own learning style. For example, if you learn better with social interaction, but the instructor teaches with lectures only, start a study group or create a group activity that will help you learn the material better.

Here's another example: The instructor or trainer uses a lot of visuals to present new material, but listening is easier for you. Perhaps start a dialogue about the material, with peers and colleagues, or ask the instructor to explain the visual aids in greater detail for clarification.

It's important to be aware of your own preferences so you can use that as a strength. Then you're able to focus on the material based on your own learning style.

PROFESSIONAL DEVELOPMENT

It's best to start thinking about your professional growth early, so you can take it step by step and enjoy the journey. Seeking training and building professional skills can start in college but will continue throughout your career. Learning new skills and new information about your field can be enriching and empowering. You start to become an expert in your area of knowledge and can really build from there. Professional development opportunities include internships, volunteer work, specialized training, conferences, professional certificates, reading books about your field, networking with your colleagues or connecting with a mentor you can learn from, and getting involved in professional clubs or organizations. This personal growth takes on many different forms. Discover what works best for you. If you feel motivated and interested in what you're learning, then you're on the right track.

Keep in mind, your career is a journey that will evolve over time. For example, college students change their major on average three times while they are in school, and working people change their careers on average seven times over their lifetime. One occupation can work great for someone for a period of time, but they may eventually find something different for the next season in their life. It's important to stay open and flexible. Think of it as an exploration process, where you are discovering more about yourself, your likes, dislikes, skills, values and many more personal attributes. Learning new things opens our mind and possibilities in our lives.

I'm grateful for my past work experience, as I learned customer service working in retail, then in food service while in college. I took those skills with me to the next job and then the next one after that. I gained instructional and leadership skills as a teacher. Then working in student services at the college and law school levels helped me to build my organizational and event-planning skills. I became very detail-oriented to build accuracy in my work performance. Working in college admissions helped me build my knowledge and strategy, so I'm able to help students prepare for applying to college and graduate school. As a counselor, I'm able to pull on all my past experiences to better support college students and young professionals in their success. My field of work requires skills that include active listening and cultural sensitivity, so that I can offer appropriate and effective resources and strategies. You can see where the skills build up and ultimately are helpful with future professional endeavors.

Back to you. There are many student clubs and organizations on a college campus that can help you build your network, gain skills in your field, and get learning opportunities. It is the same with other organizations at the career level after college. One connection can lead to another, and to another from there. Before you know it, you've created new and exciting opportunities for yourself.

LIFELONG LEARNING

College and vocational training may happen for people at different times in their lives. Gone are the days that it must happen right after high school, and you must finish college by a certain age. People of all ages go back to school or training at different times in their lives. If your goal is to get it done early, great. But know that we never stop learning throughout our lives. For example, after college and/or graduate school and well into one's career, one might decide to learn a new skill or trade or even a new hobby. Learning is all about growth and enjoyment. Even if you're all settled in your career and are happy with it, it's mentally healthy to keep learning new things, even if it's just for fun. Therefore, challenge yourself and have fun with it!

I've heard people say we change every seven to ten years over our lifetime. What actually changes really depends on the person and their own experiences. When I started thinking about what my life was like seven to ten years ago, I realized how different it was. Even my way of thinking and perspective has changed over time. This is normal and healthy. Our personal experiences really do shape who we become, and it's a beautiful natural transformation that happens. Allow both the good and bad experiences to help you learn and grow. We can gain gratitude from the positive ones and resilience and wisdom from the negative ones.

Your reason for learning, and the things you are interested in learning about, are unique to you. Everyone has a different journey. Embrace your own! I've heard people say traveling is educational, and I agree. I love to travel and feel that this experience is always different for me. I gain a new perspective each time I go somewhere new. The same goes with reading for fun. Are you getting the picture of what lifelong learning is about? Your education and career are just a part of that. But it is a big part, so choose wisely and really commit yourself to it. I will never stop learning. I want to practice my Spanish speaking skills. I want to learn to play the guitar. I really enjoy trainings and conferences to learn about new things going on in my own profession. If it has to do with something we're passionate about, it will feel more like enjoyment rather than work. So never stop learning and enjoy the journey.

> "If you are not willing to learn, no one can help you. If you are determined to learn, no one can stop you" (EDITION, 2021).
>
> —Zig Ziglar, author, salesman, and motivational speaker

Does this sound interesting to you? Well, keep reading then, to learn tips and strategies for studying and training so you can become your very best self in work, in school, and in life.

HOW TO LEARN BETTER (TRAINING AND STUDY SKILLS)

This is what Maya Angelou said when referring to her life and it resonates with me so deeply.

"I did then what I knew how to do. Now that I know better, I do better" (Belmont, 2019).

—Maya Angelou, memoirist, poet, and civil rights activist

When I meet with clients or students, I always want to offer them my best. I want to show up prepared to offer them what they need in order to move forward in their lives. I'll never be perfect, but I try to find ways to improve and sharpen my skills and build my knowledge. This can start in college or vocational school (pre-career). In fact, college is really where you start building your career. It's your area of study and expertise. It's also the building of relationships and connections with your future colleagues. It's the experiences you have in extracurricular activities that you can tailor to support your career. The same thing goes for those already in the workplace. You are learning from other colleagues, and they are learning from you. Seek opportunities for further development, like training and professional conferences. You may be really good at what you do for work, but there's always room for growth and improvement. Continue to challenge yourself to learn new things.

Still in school and/or professional training? Here are some learning tips for you.

Class notes, reading notes, projects/assignments, exams:

When you are sitting in class listening and watching a lecture, pay attention and grasp the main ideas being presented, and write notes as important things come up. Usually, the instructor will hint around to what part of the material is the most important to understand. Feeling like you have to catch everything or write down each and everything being said will hinder you from really absorbing the right information. There's a difference between trying to memorize everything and really understanding it. When class is over, it takes about twenty minutes to start forgetting what you just heard, so it's a good idea to take some time right after class to review your class notes and add what you remember to your notes. You will be able to recall things you didn't get a chance to write down during class. The more time that goes by, the harder it will be to recall information. If you put it off until later, you will most likely forget important details to add. Reviewing your class notes right after class aids in the process of understanding and retaining new information.

Same thing goes for reading assignments. As you read on your own, try to understand the main topic(s) and stop along the way to write your own reading notes. In your own words, summarize what you've just read and write it down. By putting it in your own words, it helps you to understand the new information, and by writing it down, it helps you to remember it. It's nice to be able to easily recall the information when you take an exam in class because you've taken the time to study and review.

Also, approach each assignment or project as an opportunity to learn more about what will be on the next test. Try your best on each assignment and that very effort will help you test well. It's about living the experience rather than memorizing information. You'll just forget it all after regurgitating it all on an exam if you're just memorizing. And what are you really learning? How to pass a test? How to barely get by in life? The knowledge we gain and build on contributes to our future in many ways.

We can remember a lot of things, especially if we take brain breaks. Studying one subject for an hour and then taking a break is helpful. Our brains need space and time to absorb new information, so we can continue to learn more and not get overloaded. When there's too much going on in our minds, we're more likely to forget information.

Every so often, be sure to review all your notes throughout the semester. A suggestion is to review the last lecture notes, again, right before the next class session to remind yourself of what was covered in the last class. Again, you're trying to build on your knowledge little by little. This is the best way to absorb it. It's a terrible feeling, trying to cram all the information into your brain the night before an important exam. Procrastination is not your friend. (see Chapter 1 for best time management tips.) Keep in mind, we tend to forget things we don't regularly review. So review, review, review . . . and you will be best prepared for assignments and tests.

The following are the common notetaking methods, but you can adopt or create your own. Remember to use your personal learning style you read about earlier in this chapter. Every person has their own learning style and their own challenges. So your approach will be unique.

Cornell Method by Walter Pauk and Ross Owens J. Q. (2010)

Key Points	Your Class Notes

Summary

T-Method—variation of the original Cornell Method

Your Notes

Summary	Questions

Discussion Columns—yet another variation

Questions	Professor's Comments	Student Comments

I am a visual learner, so I tend to draw pictures and diagrams showing relation between topics. I learn better when I can make connections between things and see a pattern in the information. But all learners can start with writing down key points and later going back and filling in additional information you recall from those key points. Rewriting your notes helps to reorganize the information in your brain. This is where you can rewrite them based on your own personal learning style. Find out what works best for you. You might come up with your own notetaking method. I say go for it and try it out.

What does the brain do with incoming information?

- Builds on prior knowledge
- Seeks patterns
- Seeks meaning
- Seeks to condense
- Seeks to order and organize

Passive learning vs. active learning:

Passive learning is, for example, just reading over your notes and then walking away from them and not thinking about them again. Whereas active learning is doing something with your notes, being proactive about the information you're responsible for knowing, whether at school or work. Think about your own learning style or styles. Use your notes to learn in the way that suits you best. If you're a verbal or social learner, you might create a study group so you can discuss topics from class. If you are a logical learner, for example, maybe gather all the detailed facts and statistics about the topic in order to help you take in the information better. It's what you do with your class notes and reading notes that makes the difference. Another example of active learning is getting tutoring for any subjects you might struggle with. College campuses offer free tutoring services to students in almost all subjects, such as writing, math, science and computer courses. In addition, take advantage of any college skills workshops offered. Take workshops on various success topics such as time management, choosing a major, study tips, online learning strategies and more. These can give you helpful tips that can support your success. Look for support programs on your college campus based on your needs. There are programs that provide additional services to students who work and are parents, students from low-income families, students with disabilities, student military veterans, career and transfer programs and more. These are meant to help students succeed by providing mentorship and specific resources to meet their needs.

Learning in the workplace:

Hopefully you work or will work for a supportive institution that invests in training their staff and supports their professional development. If not, you can always seek training outside of work. Just be sure to let your employer know as you complete more training and attend any workshops or conferences. This way they see you are working on growing in your profession. Also, let your employer know about your accomplishments, praises, and compliments. It's important they value your effort and contributions.

If your employer does offer training, be sure to take advantage of every opportunity you can to learn and grow in your field. This is a lifelong effort that hopefully you will find interesting and motivating—usually one does if they are in a career they care about. More on finding a career that aligns with who "you truly are" in Chapter 5.

When attending staff meetings and training courses be sure to take notes and review them often. This will help you build on your knowledge base. Perhaps you will have new and helpful ideas you want to share with others that will help them in their growth as well.

If there is an area you want to develop in, but the opportunities don't land in your lap, go ahead and volunteer to help on a project. Challenge yourself! It's an opportunity to learn and grow. These are steps to get you where you want to go in your career. You're also building your resume with new experiences, responsibilities, and accomplishments. People will take notice when you go above and beyond your typical job duties. To balance this approach, be sure to take initiative in moderation based on the work culture. You don't want to step on any toes either. Observe and be aware first. Then proceed accordingly. You also don't want to have too much on your plate that you are overwhelmed with and can't do a good job. Balance it out. Your efforts to learn in the workplace will get noticed.

Remember that whether you're a college student or a professional just starting off, or even both, we are all on a learning journey in life. Be patient with yourself and others. The only way to success is taking chances and making mistakes along the way. These are just giant steps in learning how to do it right. Don't be discouraged when starting a new job. Learning takes time and practice. Before you know it, you get the hang of things, and soon you become the expert.

> "Expect to make some mistakes when you try new and different approaches. Sometimes colossal failures lead to spectacular successes" (Mackay, 2024).
>
> —Harvey Mackay, businessman, author, and syndicated columnist

Do you want to find out how to choose a good career for yourself or determine if the career you've already stepped into suits you well? The next chapter is meant to guide you in choosing a career that is a good fit for you, for the long term. My definition of what is a good-fit career is if you feel fulfilled at the end of the workday and on an ongoing basis doing the work you do. And I don't mean it doesn't come with challenges. I mean, despite the challenges and setbacks that come along, it is overall meaningful to you. The work you do is rewarding. A good-fit career is also one that meets your financial needs. You of course want to be able to meet your basic needs but also be comfortable, so you are not struggling to pay bills. A good-fit career also allows you to use your skills and follow your values. The next chapter is all about learning more about you and who you are so you can plan your future and create a career and life you love!

CHAPTER 5

Design Your Future

Career and life planning can be a fun process. You may be a high school student, a college student, a graduate, a young professional, or just someone wanting to change your career in any season of your life. Regardless of your life stage, this chapter will help you focus on a profession that aligns with who you truly are. It's important to be open and flexible as you approach this process. It takes each step in this chapter to get the full benefits of landing on a major (area of study) and/or career that is right for you.

Something that I've paid attention to while traveling the world is how people live and work—the happiness of some and the unhappiness of others. I can't help but ask why. Why are some people happy with the work they do to make a living while others are so miserable with their work? What I've gathered is that it's all about a person's attitude to life. I know some jobs are tougher than others but our attitude regarding work can be very powerful.

Let me explain with one simple example. As an American, I know the cultural norms and points of view well because I've lived in the U.S. my whole life. The American culture places an emphasis on your station in life and labels it with a certain value based on how much money you make or what your lifestyle looks like in terms of possessions—size of your house, income bracket, cost of your car, designer clothing, etcetera. The symbols we see growing up make us believe that having more is better and making a lot of money will make us happy. But there are plenty of people who are financially successful, who may have fancy degrees and the status they've always worked for, who still find themselves unhappy. The people who are truly happy are the people who come to realize there are more important things in life, like peace, health, and loving relationships. Everyone values different things, but regardless of what is important to us, our own attitude can change how we experience life. In my travels to South America, Europe, and Asia, I've seen people working in roles that Americans would deem less than desirable, according to our culture, like running a meat market, farming, or waiting tables. But what I see in these places are people who take pride in their work and feel fulfilled with their purpose in life. Their sense of accomplishment beams out of them no matter their socioeconomic status. I have asked myself many times, how is this so different than back home?

We need to shift our way of thinking about work and purpose. Find things to be grateful for in the present moment. This continuous gratitude just brings more happiness and contentment. Keep that in mind when you come across possible occupations in your search for a new career that may be different than you thought you would do. We need to stop believing the stereotypes about certain jobs and just be open. Try not to make assumptions right away because you could end up passing one up that would be perfect for you. Be open to learning about different options. Now, I'm not saying you need a simple job. I'm merely giving you a different perspective about the world of work. Not everyone needs to be working in a big corporation to be deemed successful. If you end up in a job that contributes to society in good ways, and it meets your needs, then all that matters is what you think and how you feel about it. Others can save their opinions for their own journey.

I have met many college students who feel pressured by their families to pursue one career or education over another. This is hard to see, especially when the student clearly doesn't want to go down that path. It's hard to succeed when you are disinterested. If you are in a career or job right now because you must be, rather than wanting to be, there are still ways to find solace in your current work. For example, try to find the positives. Does it help you reach your financial goals? Have you met nice people at work? What are some substantial things you've learned by working in this job? Is this a permanent or temporary job for you? Can you look for another job in the meantime? Remember, our attitude about life can make a difference in how we experience it.

Let's focus on the good things rather than the bad things. The bad things will remain bad for a time, whether we think about them or not. Worrying doesn't make a bad situation better. So, we might as well try to live well and work to do something about it. The following quote by the theologian, Reinhold Niebuhr, comes to mind: "God, grant me the serenity to accept the things I cannot change, the courage to change the things I can, and the wisdom to know the difference" (Morris, 2014). This quote really hits home for me. A lot of the time we think we can control everything in our lives, but it is often not the case. Then what? How do we cope when things don't go our way? We can still maintain our happiness and gain success in life. Yes, it's true. The following quote explains the law of attraction, and it resonates with me every time I come across it: "Your mind is a magnet. If you think of blessing, you attract blessings. If you think of problems, you attract problems. Always cultivate good thoughts and remain positive" (Canfield 2007).

I also believe this to be true for how we behave and how we treat others. Whatever you put out into the universe will return to you. So, send good vibes and do positive things out there, and you will attract more of those things in your life.

I want to empower you to create. You can create the life you want, starting with your profession. A career is not just a job. It is your life's work. This should be something you really care about and are interested in growing and developing in. You'll know when you land on the right one for yourself because you'll be really motivated and excited about it. One way to approach it is to ask yourself, "What is my mission in life?" Some things may come to mind, like building a home or having a family. Maybe it's learning to play an instrument or creating something significant. Maybe it is helping the community in some way. Take the time to really give it some thought and write down your ideas.

The world is full of challenges and problems that need to be solved. What challenge are you interested in solving as you contribute to society? Hector Garcia and Francesc Miralles explain it well in their book *Ikigai: The Japanese Secret to a Long and Happy Life*. Ikigai is pronounced eye-key-guy (Garcia, Miralles 2017). This concept refers to having a "challenge mindset" to find your purpose in life. Think of the needs of society. What issues do you care about enough to help and solve in society? Have a brainstorming session with people who know you well. Maybe a family member or close friend. These people usually know your natural strengths, and you can bounce ideas off them. You might even get compliments on something you do well. Listen to those because in them you will find your talents you can give to the world. When I was first starting my career as a teacher, my coworkers would say, "You have a lot of patience with kids and their parents. You are kind. You are a good listener. You should write a book someday." Depending on personality, we tend to not notice our strengths but might focus on our weaknesses instead. Afterall, our culture teaches us to improve and be better, to be competitive. However, I believe that what is already in us just needs a little direction and refining in order to bloom. We already have something in us that we truly care about in life; we already have something to offer the world that is needed. We have our gifts! It's a matter of finding out what these gifts are.

Below is a chart created by Career Connection at Ohio Wesleyan University, with societal challenges to consider. This is a good place to start and will get you thinking about different career options (Wesleyan, 2018).

CHALLENGE MINDSET CARDS

Review the challenges, descriptions, and sample job titles below and select your top three choices. Knowing what challenge, you want to tackle will aid you in thinking critically about your career, researching potential employers, and finding job opportunities that resonate with you!

Challenge	Description	Sample Job Titles
Redesign the Health Care System	Find new and innovative ways to offer better health services to more people at lower costs & prevent health problems.	Doctor, Nurse, Physiotherapist, Health Research, Healthcare Manager, Epidemiologist, Data Analyst, Policy Officer, Programmer
Promote Healthy Living	Help change people's behaviors, make an impact on the food industry, and transform government policy to promote healthy living.	Dietitian, Nutritionist, Fitness Coach, Personal Trainer, Therapist, Doctor, Public Health Promotor, Health Analyst, Scientist/ Researcher
Advance Health Informatics	Improve the acquisition, sharing, protection, and analysis of health info to improve health care delivery & stop the spread of disease.	Biostatistician, Data Scientist Epidemiologist, Software Engineer, Information Analyst, Project Manager, Business Architect, Consultant
Engineer Better Medicine	Develop systems to use genetic information, detect changes in the body, create and assess new drugs, and produce specific vaccines.	Geneticist, Pharmacist, Biologist, Chemist, Pharmacologist, Biomedical Engineer, Clinical Specialist, Health Technologist

Improve Mental Health	Educate, de-stigmatize, prevent, heal, and rehabilitate those affected by mental health issues.	Psychologist, Psychiatrist, Counselor, Therapist, Social Worker, Nurse, Researcher, Public Health/Policy Officer
Distribute the Wealth	Improve social programs to help individuals come out of poverty and impact laws/policies and innovative models to distribute wealth.	Policy Analyst, Advocate, Community Organizer, Politician, Professor, Wealth Managers, Investment Advisors, Venture Capitalist
Foster Sustainable Development	Help countries achieve their human and economic potential; economic growth, food security, human rights, health, etc.	Program Manager, Fundraiser, Proposal Writer, Foreign Service Officer, Diplomat, Policy Analyst, Researcher, Activist
Establish Fair Trade	Update or create new international agreements for fair trade so countries can exchange products and services fairly.	Economist, Negotiator, Lawyer, Trade Commissioner, Supply Chain Manager, Logistics Coordinator, Import/Export Coordinator
Entrepreneurship	Identify challenges, conduct research, create prototypes, and sell solutions to solve unmet needs.	Not limited to specific titles, education programs, fields, or career paths
Prepare Future Leaders	Equip future leaders with skills such as communication, coaching, delegation, influence, etc. to solve big problems.	Trainer/Facilitator, Coach, Human Resources Officer, Learning and Development Specialist, Consultant, Leadership Specialist
Create Artificial Intelligence	Create and use new AI to tackle the world's greatest problems, and use it to improve quality of life, education, and health.	Software Developer, Computer Engineer, User Experience Designer, Cognitive Scientist, Data Analyst, Machine Learning Researcher

Invent New Biotechnology	Provide breakthrough products to combat debilitating and rare diseases, reduce our environmental footprint, and fight poverty.	Biologist, Biotechnologists, Microbiologist, Bacteriologist, Molecular Bioengineer, Biochemist, Chemical Engineer, Laboratory Tech
Collect & Use Big Data	Collect, store, analyze, interpret, and present information from big data to provide insights to improve our lives and make predictions.	Data Scientist, Engineer/ Analyst, Business Intelligence Engineer, Solutions Architect, Statistician, Analytics, Machine Scientist
Advance Virtual Reality	Improve VR tech and software and create games & experiences in medicine, education, sports, entertainment, etc.	Software Developer, System Analyst, 3D Modeler, Engineer, Program Manager, VR Specialist/Consultant, Quality Assurance
Reverse Engineer The Brain	Enhance our true mental potential and improve people's lives through tools such as ear implants, artificial retinas, and limbs.	Neuroscientist, Neuropsychologist, Neurologist, Researcher, Professor, Scientist
Build the School of the Future	Help schools adapt to meet evolving needs and tailor learning to individuals & use advanced technologies.	Teacher, Principle, Educational Consultant, Curriculum Writer, Instructional Designer, Test Developer, School District Administrator
Protect Society From Crime	Create a safer world, and use data for predictive policing, change our rehabilitation practices, and create/update laws.	Lawyer, Judge, Politician, Criminologist, Police, Correctional Officer, Detective, Criminal Intelligence, Fraud Investigator, Security Analyst

Help People Reach Their Potential	Research human potential, learn what works best, and help individuals/groups improve and find opportunities for them to shine.	Teacher, Mentor, Tutor, Leader, Coach, Trainer, Human Resources Specialist, Social Worker, Psychologist, Counselor, Therapist, Researcher
End Extreme Poverty	Create the conditions necessary for people to thrive and address issues that contribute to poverty, such as diseases and education.	Economist, Public Relations, Logistics Coordinator, Policy/Advocacy Advisers, Project Manager, Logistics, Education/Health Specialists
Foster Understanding & Respect	Develop a better understanding, respect, and collaboration between different groups of people to shift power imbalances.	Spokesperson, Advocate, Mediator, Politician, Researcher, Public Relations Specialist, Conflict Resolution Specialist, Program Coordinator
Increase Sustainable Energy	Improve energy through research, creating new technology and tools, and promoting the use of sustainable energies.	Scientists, Environmental Engineer, Project Manager, Designer, Wind-Farm Developer, Solar Fabricator, Wave Energy Producers
Protect Biodiversity/ Landscape	Research best approaches for conserving the planet, taking care of animals, development of nature reserves, and educating the public.	Scientists, Wildlife Biologist, Zoologist, Paleontologist, Climatologist, Ecologist, Geographer, Meteorologists, Oceanographer
Design Future of Transportation	Change the way we transport materials, travel long distances, utilize airways for travel, and assist with innovative solutions.	Urban Planner, Transportation Engineer, Safety Engineer, Operations Manager, Researcher, Transport Planner, Pilot, Traffic Management

Manage the Planet's Waste	Recover wasted resources and develop a "reprocessing" industry to transform valuable resources to be used by the world.	Waster Engineer, Biofuel Specialist, Sustainability Consultant, Social Responsibility Manager, Hydrologist, Hydrogeologist
Create New Food & Food Systems	Produce and promote superfoods and alternative protein sources to encourage healthy eating and minimize waste.	Urban Growers, Agriculture & Food Scientists, Food Inventor, Forester, Microbiologist, Molecular Biologist, Chef, Entomologists
Communicate Ideas & Emotions	Use creativity to tell stories and inspire action to help people/ organizations deliver a clear, inspiring, and human message.	Storyteller, Editor, Branding Specialist, Data Analyst, Film/Video Editor, Research Analyst, Photographer, Writer, Social Media Strategist
Master Tools & Machines	Work with tool and machines to problem solve and use creativity to help build, organize, improve, drive, and repair things.	Mechanic, Engineer, Technician, Plumber, Robot Operator, Installation Expert, Electrician, Automotive Specialist, Construction Professional
Create Meaningful Experiences for Others	Help others feel heard, understood, and supported in their goals and connected to a community by asking questions, listening, and finding solutions.	Sales Representative, Store Manager, Client Services Coordinator, User Experience Designer, Customer Service Rep, Retail Manager, Health Care Worker
Inspire Through Art	Give a voice to the voiceless, reflect the human experience, and help people think critically about themselves and environments.	Animator, Illustrator, Graphic Designer, Art Therapist, Painter, Sculptor, Museum Curator, Arts Administrator, Interior Designer

Choosing a career also involves creating the lifestyle you want in the future. What does your future look like in your heart? What is important to you? The career you choose today should align with what this looks like for you. There are many factors to consider, but here are a few questions to consider:

- What are your strengths?
- How much money do you want to make?
- How much flexibility or autonomy do you want?

It always comes down to what is important to you, and it helps to have this in mind while building your career. I want to give you some food for thought by sharing the following passage by Viktor Frankl, in his book *Man's Search for Meaning*:

> A statistical survey of 7,948 students at forty-eight colleges was conducted by social scientists from Johns Hopkins University. Their preliminary report is part of a two-year study sponsored by the National Institute of Mental Health. Asked what they considered "very important" to them now, 16 percent of the students checked "making a lot of money"; 78 percent said their first goal was finding a purpose and meaning to my life. (Frankl 2006, 100)

Although most students prioritized finding a purpose, some placed the focus on making a lot of money. Maybe these students will shift their focus later in life, or maybe not. Either way, it's important for them to also find meaning and purpose in life, and it's more than just making a lot of money. Maybe it's making a lot of money for them to be able to help their family.

You will need to discover what is important and meaningful to you. Self-reflection and exploration are the first steps. Plus, they're fun! This includes assessing your personality type and what your preferences are in a work environment. It also includes exploring your interests and being aware of your personal strengths and skills acquired. It's important to also know your values, what you deeply care about in life. All these personal attributes ought to be considered when planning your career and life.

If you find yourself feeling lost and don't know where to start or which route to take when it comes to your career or major, you can seek help from a career counselor. A career counselor can help you through the self-reflection and career exploration process. The important thing is to know yourself before making any big commitments. Luckily, you have this book in your hands, and it will help guide you.

YOUR SELF-REFLECTION AND WHO YOU ARE

There are many assessment questionnaires you can take to understand your personality type, interests, strengths, skills, and values. These are all important factors to take into consideration first, before choosing your career. Every person will have different reasons for choosing one career over another, but it will be more beneficial to consider these personal factors first. Again, you can gain access to these assessments by speaking with a career counselor, but below are some sources if you decide you would like to start the process on your own:

- CareerOneStop.org (assess your interests, skills, and work values, search career database)
- Truity.com (The Big Five Personality Test)
- Gallup.com (Strengths Finder 2.0 assessment) This can also be found on Amazon.
- MyNextMove.org (career interest assessment and database of occupations)

Take the above assessments to find out more about how unique you are. Self-awareness will allow you to move forward in your career development more intentionally. Once you gather your results of the assessments you take, you can use this information to search for different careers that align with your personal attributes. Writing down the main takeaways of the assessments' results, in a chart or in your journal, will be helpful as you search for your next career. The purpose of this is to find a career that is a good fit for you and will bring you long-term job satisfaction. Both CareerOneStop.org and MyNextMove.org also have a search engine where you can find occupations that match your personal attributes based on your assessment results. These are good tools you can use to start a list of potential careers you're interested in. Below is a sample chart to help you put it all together:

Find a career that fits the important factors below. Input your assessments' results.

Your Personal Traits	Notes
Personality:	
Interests:	

Skills/Strengths:

Work Values:

Ask yourself the following questions.

Working Conditions: What physical work surroundings feel good to me and help me to do my best work? Inside or outside? Windows? Size of organization or department? Dress code? Supervision? Etcetera.

Compromise: If I must, which of the above could I compromise? What would I be willing to give up in order to get the job I want? This could be a certain skill, work condition, or work value.

Career Options: What are my top career options that are the best fit for me currently? You may want to save this response for later, after you do some research.

Read on to discover how to start your career search.

SEARCHING FOR CAREER OPTIONS

Based on the results of your assessments, you can find ideas for careers or majors that would be a good fit while you research different options. For example, on the CareerOneStop.org site, you can search for occupations based on your interests and based on your skills to get some ideas. There is a tool for this on their site. It leads to many different occupations to consider based on your personal traits. Start checking things out and see if you like anything. You might stumble upon something you weren't even thinking about but would really love. Another site is O*NetOnline.org. Here you can browse occupations by your abilities, interests, knowledge, skills, work activities, work context, work styles, and work values. Both CareerOneStop.org and O*Net online are sponsored by the U.S. Department of Labor, Employment and Training Administration.

If you have a little more life experience and want to search for careers based on your education and/or work experience, you can use the Crosswalk feature at O*NetOnline.org. Here you will be able to search for occupations by education level, work, skills, or military experience, etcetera.

One other tool on the O*Net site is searching for careers by Job Families. If you have a sense of the industry or field you're interested in but don't know any occupations in this field, you can search by a Job Family first. This will generate a list of occupations in that field.

Once you've done some research on these sites and find career options you want to further consider, make a list of three to five careers you find interesting. Then go to the *Occupational Outlook Handbook* at bls.gov/ooh/. This is the U.S. Bureau Labor Statistics database, where you can find career information as it pertains to salary by state or county, job outlook, work environment, duties, and tasks for each of the careers on your list of prospects. When using this tool with my clients, a few of them have created a chart to keep track of the information. It's up to you how you want to gather the information that you're learning about. Maybe it just lives in your brain, and you can easily download it like a computer. I'm impressed!

As you search different occupations in the *Occupational Outlook Handbook*, O*NetOnline.org, CareerOneStop.org, and MyNextMove.org sites, see below for important things to keep in mind and take note of:

- Role and level of responsibility of job
- Tasks and duties on a day-to-day basis
- Work alone or with others
- Skills and knowledge needed
- Technical skills needed
- Salary amount by state or county you will live in (it's different across the nation)
- Job outlook: Will there be job growth in the coming years? How many of these jobs are projected to be available?
- Education and training needed
- Does the job align with your personality, interests, strengths/skills, and values?
- Does this career fit the lifestyle you want to create, and does it allow for the life roles that are important to you? (more on this later)
- What other related occupations exist in your field of interest?

On the notion of being open and flexible, your career choice at this time may serve you well for a season and may eventually evolve over time, based on your life stages and personal experiences. Think about the stages we go through at different ages throughout our life. According to Donald E. Super, a psychologist who contributed a lot to career development theory, the life stages include Growth (ages 14 and under), Exploration (14–25), Establishment (26–45), Maintenance (46–65) and Disengagement (65 and upward). These are typical age ranges but can vary. In fact, someone who is in their forties and wants a career change can go through the "Exploration" stage again (Super, 1957). So, this is fluid and is really based on the individual.

Now think about all the roles you will have over your lifetime while going through these stages. Typical ones include child (until parents are deceased), student, "leisurite," citizen, worker, parent, spouse, homemaker (creating your own home, no longer living with parents). In Super's theory of psychology of careers, he explains how career development intersects with the many roles an individual will play throughout their life and the different life stages they go through (Super 1981). This is also known as the Career Life Rainbow (see diagram below). The theory explains how our self-concept changes over time with new and different experiences. We go through different life-stages and roles, affecting how much time we have to spend on work, play, family, etcetera. As life changes, we need to still be able to create balance so that we may effectively play our roles.

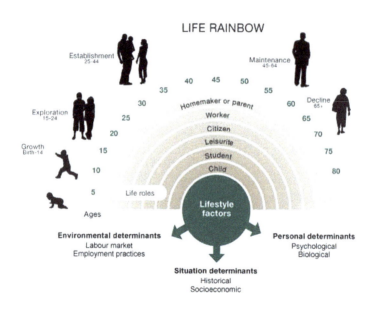

(SUPER, ADAPTED 1981)

According to this theory and my current lived experience, I am in the "Maintenance" life stage in the diagram above. I'll share my current life roles with you below, so you have some examples. These are in no particular order.

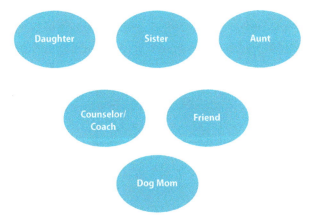

Now, it's your turn. In the ovals below input your current life roles. Feel free to add more.

What is your current life-stage (refer to Life Rainbow above)? _____

This is a good exercise, my friend. As you search and explore different majors and careers, be sure to go back to this to always keep your roles and commitments in mind and align your career decisions around the roles that are important to you. You don't want to step into a job that causes stress to any of your life roles. Keep in mind, certain roles will change over time, and you will take on new life roles in the future. How do your career goals fit in your life currently? How will your goals fit in your future life roles? Have fun with your career search, and really take the time to learn about your options and tailor your plans to suit you best.

After you have conducted your career research, narrowed down your career options to one or two serious considerations, the next step is to further explore these one or two careers. At this point you'll have some pretty good options. The goal here is to narrow down your choices even more to allow space for the next step of career exploration. Ponder which ones you want to really dive into and learn more about.

One thing to keep in mind that is important is the need to be adaptable. We live in a time that requires us to be fluid in our mindset and our approach to career development because of all the changes in technology, in societal challenges or problems, and what remains needed out there. Please don't feel like you'll be married to this career forever. It is a foundation that you're building upon that will eventually grow and sprout into other opportunities and career pivots. It's okay. Just follow your heart and go with the flow and be adaptable. More and more employers are seeking individuals who can come on board and fulfill the required roles and tasks of a particular season based on their needs.

Be open and your hard work and solid work ethic will pay off. Eventually, you will be able to create the work and career that you're happy with for the long term. This will be your life's work. This goal is what motivates you to work hard to grow and contribute to your field. This is what you really care about in life. As discussed earlier, the Japanese call this reason for being ikigai. Below is a helpful diagram as you envision your career life. Notice that ikigai is in the center. This is comparable to your "why."

(GARCIA, MIRALLES, 2017)

EXPLORING A CAREER, YOU'RE INTERESTED IN

This next step is vital and requires more time; that's why it's a good idea to only have one or two options at this point. It's one thing to read about different careers online but quite another to actually see what they are like in real life. Below are some ideas for things you can do in order to learn more about your top career interests.

- Informational interviewing: You can seek the advice of people in those careers by asking to meet with someone who works in a role you are interested in. Have some of your burning questions ready. More on this later.
- Shadow someone at work for a day to see what it is really like to be in that role.
- Volunteer to work in your field of interest to learn more about it.

- Internships, temporary assignments, or part-time work in the field build valuable experience.
- Entry-level work: This gets your foot in the door and allows you to learn all aspects of the field from the bottom up.
- Meet people in the field and learn more by going to professional conferences and trainings.
- Start to connect with professionals in your field of interest via LinkedIn.
- Seek out a free introductory course or workshop online where you can learn more about the skills needed.

This career exploration stage should help you learn more about the career you are considering. You will gain information beyond what you can read about online. Some people are convinced they want to pursue a certain career, and once they get hands-on experience, they realize it's not for them after all. Save yourself some time in the beginning to discover what works for you. You will feel much more confident in your career choice. This will lead you to the next big step in the process, deciding on your career and/or major choice.

I wanted to share some key tips with you about informational interviewing. You might know someone who is working in a role that you're interested in doing. Or you might know of someone who can introduce you to someone they know in that role. If so, great! You can reach out to your connections to ask if you can meet with them. If you don't already have a connection in the field or the role you're interested in, then you'll need to make a new connection. I suggest searching on LinkedIn for someone who is already working in this role and request a connection and/or a private message through LinkedIn. Introduce yourself and let them know you're just starting off and would like to learn more about their career. Always be kind and appreciative. I know you will be! They might reply and offer to speak with you about it. If they are responsive, awesome. You can also ask if they would be willing to talk with you for thirty minutes about their job and how they got there. Be open to a phone or video call or an in-person meeting. Make it easy and convenient for them.

Before meeting with the person, think about the questions you still have about this type of work after researching it thoroughly. Do your research before. This way, the questions you still have are thoughtful and meaningful ones. Write them down and have them ready for your meeting. Also allow space for the person to explain in their own words about their personal experience working in the field. Let them talk and see what they share. They may answer your questions before you ask them. And the more you allow them to share, the more pearls of wisdom you'll get from them.

Be at the meeting on time and be sensitive to how long the meeting takes. You don't want to go over the thirty minutes you asked for. Wrap up the meeting on time and thank them for their time and valuable insight. Have your resume ready to give them after the meeting as well. You will be making a professional connection. They may really like you and want to keep you in mind for opportunities in the future. Having your resume up to date and ready to offer it will be helpful.

Remember, you are seeking their advice, so sending a thank-you gift card is always a nice touch. For example, I've used a $10 Starbucks gift card before. If you can't afford a gift, no problem. Just a thank-you card will do. The benefits from an informational interview include making a meaningful connection to the world you want to work in. You get your burning questions answered from someone with first-hand experience. You get even more information than you expected or than you can read about online. You learn more about the career you're interested in, to see if it's a good fit for you. You are putting yourself out there and planting a seed that can grow and bloom into opportunities for you later. Go for it.

After you have taken these steps to further explore your career with the various suggestions above, it will be time to decide if you will make this career a goal of yours.

DECIDING ON YOUR MAJOR AND/OR CAREER

To establish your goal, you'll need to decide on your career or major first. As a reminder, your career will evolve over time, so you don't have to feel the pressure of a lifelong commitment. Accomplishing this first step will lead to even greater opportunities and new ideas on your life's journey. The important thing is that you choose something you feel good about, something that you find interesting and care about. This will keep you motivated on your path to success.

Hopefully, the process of career searching based on who you are, and career exploration guides you and helps you land on one great option that you feel confident and excited about and that you can really begin to focus on. You've got this!

I want to remind you of something I mentioned earlier in this book. I shared my personal journey of being a schoolteacher, which eventually led me to a passion for counseling. I don't regret choosing to teach back then. I *loved* it! Looking back now, I realize it was a great experience for me for that time of my life. Now I am enjoying this season of my life as a counselor and coach. Remember, the process I recommend in this chapter will help you find a career that allows you to be who you were always meant to be.

> "It takes courage to grow up and become who you really are" (SportsNotebooks, 2020).
>
> —E.E. Cummings, poet, painter, essayist, author, and playwright

Take a deep breath and ponder the quote above. Look forward to the future you will create. It is yours for the taking.

Below is the Decision Checklist (created by Career Journeys) that I shared with you in Chapter 2. Go through it before you make your big decision on your major and/or career. If you can check off all the items on the list, rest assured you are making a good decision.

Item	Notes
Check in with both sides of your brain.	Find the balance between emotion and reason. It's important to factor in both logic and how you feel about it.
Visualize your future successful self.	When you have a positive mental image of your success, you begin to believe you can make it. You must believe before you can achieve.
Recognize the power behind each decision you make.	Understand the effects of your decision. Any decision you make causes a chain of events to happen.
Go with your gut.	When you find yourself wavering between two options, your intuition is one of your most powerful decision-making tools.
Don't ask people what you should do.	Having too many outside opinions can cause you to second-guess yourself. However, feel free to consult with the people who will be directly affected by your decision.
Ask yourself the right questions.	What do I want in this lifetime? Will the outcome of my decision move me closer to what I truly want? Does the benefit outweigh the cost? Is the level of risk worth the reward? How committed am I to this change?
Align your life with your core values.	Make your decisions based on whether or not they align with your highest values, passions, and priorities or it's not going to feel like you made the right choice.
Whatever you decide to do, have grit and gusto!	Make sure you're doing something that motivates you to persevere (despite failure). There's power in your passion.

(CAREER JOURNEYS, 2016)

"It is in your moments of decision that your destiny is shaped" (Lopez, 2020).

—Tony Robbins, author and motivational speaker

Your next step involves creating a SMART goal, discussed in Chapter 2. See, you are already using the tips in this book!

Create Your SMART Goal First:

SMART goals (Doran, Miller, Cunningham 1981, 35–36) are designed to help you identify whether what you want to achieve is realistic, purposeful and to determine a deadline. When writing SMART goals, use concise language but include relevant information. These are designed to help you succeed, so be positive when answering the questions. Use the following steps to help you come up with a SMART goal for your career decision.

Initial Goal (*Write the goal you have in mind*):

_____

_____

_____

_____

1. Specific (*What do you want to accomplish? Who needs to be included? When do you want to do this? Why is this a goal?*)

_____

_____

_____

_____

2. Measurable (*How can you measure progress and know if you've successfully met your goal?*):

_____

_____

_____

_____

3. Achievable *(Do you have the skills required to achieve the goal? If not, can you obtain them? What is the motivation for this goal? Is the amount of effort required on par with what the goal will achieve?):*

_____

_____

_____

_____

4. Relevant *(Why am I setting this goal now? Is it aligned with overall objectives?):*

_____

_____

_____

_____

_____

5. Time-bound *(What's the deadline, and is it realistic?):*

_____

_____

_____

_____

_____

SMART Goal *(Review what you have written, and craft a new goal statement based on what the answers to the questions above have revealed):*

_____

_____

_____

_____

CREATING YOUR ACTION PLAN

Write down your goal first. Then brainstorm how this goal is SMART (discussed in Chapter 2) by writing down the **S**pecifics of the goal, how you will **M**easure your progress, how it is **A**chievable for you, how **R**ealistic it is to make it happen in your life, and what **T**ime frame you are giving yourself to reach your goal. If this goal checks off each of the SMART goal criteria, then create steps you'll take to reach your goal. Remember to celebrate as you complete each step in your action plan. You are one step closer to your dream!

Consider the possible steps below to starting your career, as you brainstorm:

- What is the education needed, if any?
- What training is needed?
- How can I gain the work experience needed—intern/volunteer/work?
- How can I build a network of professionals who can be a support to me?
- How can I conduct a job search to get my foot in the door?
- Which key skills and knowledge are needed for my field? How will I build these skills?

Now that you have established your SMART career goal and brainstormed what your action steps might be, use the handy chart below to plan your steps to reach that goal. Be as specific as possible so you have an action plan for exactly what you will do.

State your goal: _____

Steps I Will Take Toward My Goal	Completion Date Planned for Each Step	Notes for Each Step (e.g. how this step gets me closer to my goal)
1		
2		
3		
4		
5		

Journal Prompt: What is important to me in life (personal and work)? What do I want my life's work to be?
Take a moment to give this some thought. Then write down your responses in your journal or notebook.

> "Ten years from now, make sure you can say that you chose your life, you didn't settle for it" (Giacomucci, 2024).
>
> —Mandy Hale, mother, author, and motivational speaker

When my sister and I were teenagers, about 17 and 18 years old, our dad would have these long conversations with us about the future. I could tell it came from the heart when he told us, "Someday you're going to be 30 years old. You might as well get there with a degree or two." He wanted to share how important it was to get an education. I also remember him saying "If you invest in yourself now, you will have a high return on your investment down the road. When you get your degree, no one can take that away from you. You'll always have it." He wanted us to know that the time and energy put into our hard work will pay off and be worth it. Back then a much smaller percentage of people were going to college, so it was a big deal. These talks made me believe in myself and I started to feel like I could get a college degree and do anything I set my mind to. He told us "You are just starting out your life, you can be anything you want to be!" Although I didn't have the skills to be anything, luckily, I chose something that matched my strengths and interests. His confidence in me made me feel more confident in myself. My students appreciate it when I share this with them. I can tell by their smiles. I hope that encourages you a bit regarding your career goals.

Your goal may or may not require a college degree. Whatever your goal is, invest yourself in it fully. Your hard work with pay off.

Now that you have an action plan for your SMART career goal, what will you do to market yourself so you can start gaining experience in your field? Start creating your brand now. That's right! It's never too early to start building your personal brand. This way, you'll be ready when opportunities come your way. The next chapter will give you some insight into where to start.

CHAPTER 6

Personal Branding for All of Your Awesomeness

"Personal branding begins the moment you discover yourself" (Chan, 2024).

—Bernard Kelvin Clive, author, speaker, trainer and known as Ghana's foremost authority on personal branding

Your professional summary or profile should reflect your personal branding. What is branding? Your personal and professional branding is a culmination of your values, skills, and experience that differentiates you from others. Think about what makes you unique. Write this down in your journal or notebook so you can go back to it from time to time as a reminder. What are your values, the things that are most important to you? Perhaps you are passionate about a cause or a mission. What are your skills and natural strengths? If you're not sure, you can ask friends and family who know you well. Write down their answers. Sometimes we don't see everything about ourselves that others can. What are your personal experiences that have shaped who you are today? Maybe you have a childhood experience that was significant, or maybe you discovered something about yourself while working at a particular job. Whatever it is, it is yours. What is your story? This is your life's journey so far, which has brought you to your present-day views and beliefs.

Another way to ask is, what do you stand for? Take some time to think about your *why* or your mission in life. Perhaps you feel you have a purpose. It is very important that you write this down.

> "The purpose of life is to discover your gifts. The meaning of life is to gift it away."
>
> (Van Allen, 2013) —David Viscott, psychiatrist, author, businessman, and media personality

Your brand may include anything that summarizes or reflects what you do and who you are as a professional. This chapter discusses your resume, your online bio, your job application, cover letter or letter of interest, your references, how you present yourself in a job interview, your mission, your expertise, and your professional portfolio.

But before we get to each of these pieces, let's take a look at this diagram, which generally describes personal branding:

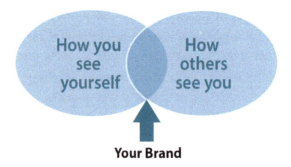

Your Brand

Your brand is how you see yourself and how others see you, both combined. The following topics will contribute to your personal and professional branding. This is important for marketing yourself to potential employers and creating the right opportunities in your network.

PUTTING YOUR RESUME TOGETHER

Your resume is a snapshot of your work-related accomplishments. This includes education and training, work and volunteer experience, special skills, extracurricular activities that align with your career goals, and your current and past roles in the workplace. While putting all of these pieces together, keep in mind it should be as concise and to the point as possible. A well-written resume will give the reader enough information about you to determine if you are qualified for the job you are applying for. If it is too lengthy, it may not be read by the hiring manager entirely. Keep it reader-friendly and you will benefit from this. Keep in mind, managers are reading a lot of resumes.

Are you writing your resume for the first time or revamping an existing one? Even if you already have a working resume, it helps to start by brainstorming first. Write down your current and past jobs with dates and make a list of your duties and tasks under each job. Once you've exhausted your tasks and duties list, go back and circle only the ones that are the most important and relevant. Which ones will help you in your next job? Take out the ones that don't. Do this under each job you've listed.

Note: If you already have some jobs you want to apply for, look at their job descriptions. See what they are looking for in a candidate. The minimum or desired qualifications area can help you tailor how you describe your tasks and duties on your resume. Sometimes, hiring managers are looking for key words. Again, these are found in the job description. This area will become the bulk of your resume. However, remind yourself to keep it concise.

Next, list your education and training. If you don't have a lot of work experience and are just starting off your career, list this toward the top of the resume right before work experience. If you have some work history, list your education and training after your jobs. If you have not yet completed your degree and/or certificate, you can still list it with an anticipated completion date, so employers know you are working on it.

Then, list any special skills you have. This can be listed after the education section. Again, if you don't have a lot of work experience, you're listing both your education and special skills toward the top of your resume right before the work experience section. If you do have significant work experience, list these two sections after the work experience. Really think about every skill you have and list them. Then you can go back and circle the ones that are the most relevant for the type of work you seek. Remove the others. A tip for this section is to not use words and phrases that are subjective but only ones that are objective. Below are some examples.

Examples of subjective skills:

- Personable
- Organized
- Detail-oriented

Examples of objective skills:

- Proficiency in a second language (list the language)
- Experience with Microsoft Office programs
- Leadership/organization training (list which ones)

You will only include the key and relevant items on your resume from your current and past job list of tasks and duties as well as your list of special skills. Again, you're only including the circled items on your resume. This helps with keeping your resume concise and impactful.

The next step is to write a list of your professional activities. Do you hold any professional memberships? Are you affiliated with any organizations in your field? Maybe you hold an office or some special role? If you're limited to your college activities, that's okay. This is just as meaningful. List any student clubs or organizations and any academic activities you are or were involved in. Volunteer work or internships are things you want to list here as well. No matter what form your professional engagement has taken, this will show a deep commitment to your line of work. It goes a long way because it shows you are willing to put in the effort and develop in your profession.

Now, I want you to think about all of your accomplishments in life so far. Make a list of these. Maybe you worked on an important project at school or at work. Maybe you helped others in some way shape or form. Maybe you led a group project that went well. Perhaps you organized an event that ran smoothly. When brainstorming about this, think about answering these questions:

- What was the situation and/or assignment?
- What action did you take?
- What were the results?

Take your answers and summarize them as briefly as possible. Quantify and qualify whenever possible.

To quantify means to include numbers or units that measure these accomplishments. For example, "After one month in this role, my sales went up by 35 percent." Another example is "After one year in my role, I was promoted to X." One last example is "I created X during my first year on the job." It's okay to include personal commitments and hobbies that show discipline, passion, etcetera.

After you have given a lot of thought to what you have accomplished, you guessed it, go back and circle the ones you feel are the most relevant to your resume at this time. Think about the types of jobs you will be applying for. What sort of skills does it take to accomplish the items on your list? Demonstrating how you have exercised these skills will speak volumes on your resume. Again, demonstrating, not telling, that you have the skills is much more effective. These accomplishments should be included in the experience section under each respective job listed that they apply to. Additionally, you can include non-work-related accomplishments under your extracurricular activities section on your resume. This section can be listed toward the bottom of the resume. What if I don't have any professional accomplishments, just hobbies, you might ask? An example of this might be someone who's played tennis their whole life. Although this is a fun and healthy activity, you can assume the person is probably competitive and enjoys a challenge. We can also gather that they persevere when things get tough, and that these are transferable skills that are useful in the workplace. They must know how to work on a skill and get better and better at it. Get where I'm going? So, your resume will tell a story of who you are and what you're capable of accomplishing.

Finally, save the summary at the top of your resume for last. Brainstorming all the above sections on your resume first should help you put some thought into your experiences. How do you want to represent yourself? What are you hoping to do next in your career? Highlight these in your summary. This is part of your professional brand. This top portion of your resume can also be titled "Professional Profile" or "Professional Summary," or "Objective." This will summarize in a phrase or sentence what you do and who you are professionally. Again, keep it short and clear. Here is a sample objective or summary. The first one is based on little experience and the second one is based on more work experience. Be sure to create your own with a statement that suits your own professional pursuits.

> *"College student with communications and leadership experience, seeking a role in marketing strategy"*

Or

> *"Marketing strategist with over 5 years of proven communication and leadership experience and success"*

Below is an outline of the items I am suggesting you include on your resume so you can see it visually.

Order of resume items for those with work experience:

- Your full name
- Summary or Profile or Objective (you choose)
- Work Experience (list current job and previous ones chronologically backwards)
- Education and Training
- Special Skills
- Professional Activities

Order of resume items for those with little to no work experience:

- Your full name
- Summary or Profile or Objective (you choose)
- Education and Training (completed or pending completion)
- Special Skills
- Professional Activities (clubs/ organizations, trainings/conferences)
- Extracurricular/co-curricular Activities (school related or hobbies/sports)
- Work Experience (list current job and previous ones chronologically backwards if applicable). You can list internships and volunteer experience as well. It's okay if you don't have any.

If you don't have a lot of work experience or have gaps of time between jobs, it's okay. It's more than okay. You've got to start somewhere. Everyone started somewhere, with very little or no work experience at all. You will gain and build your experience over time. Don't worry about it looking bad on your resume.

You can use this *chronological* resume style discussed above, or you have the option to use a *functional* resume format instead. A functional resume will highlight your experience and skills more than it does the list of jobs you've had. You can make your resume more about you and what you bring rather than about your past jobs. The key is to include only information that is relevant to the work you're pursuing currently. See yourself in your desired role and represent yourself in this role on your resume. A *functional* resume can look like the following outlined items:

- Your full name
- Professional Summary (specifically what makes you a good candidate for the role you're applying for)
- Work Experience (list your current job title on the first line, then your previous job on the second line, then the one before that on the third line etcetera. Include dates you worked in each role. Then below this, list bulleted statements describing your relevant responsibilities practiced in all the job titles listed, regardless of dates. Also include specific accomplishments here. You are including all in one area instead of breaking them up by job title. Remember to qualify and quantify whenever possible).
- Education and Training
- Special Skills
- Professional Activities

The goal with a *functional* resume is to highlight your accomplishments over your job titles, their dates, and duties. No one wants to read a comprehensive list of duties, just the relevant ones for the job you're applying for.

Note: You can google "functional resume" and see many samples of written ones for ideas. You can also google "chronological resume," so you can compare and see the difference.

After you have written your summary at the top of your resume, described your work experience and accomplishments, and included your education and training, special skills, and professional activities on your resume, be sure to input your contact information right after your name at the top so it's easy to find. But only list your phone number and email—no need to include your physical address.

Just a few basic tips for your overall resume: Stick to one font style and one font size throughout the document (font size 11 or 12). Use the bold font option for your name and headlines and the regular font for the rest. Using too many sizes and fonts can be overwhelming for the eye or can look unprofessional. Keep it clean and simple. Your resume should be one page in length.

Now, walk away from the resume and take a break for a while to refresh your focus. Then come back to it later to proofread the whole resume and adjust as you see fit. Then have a second pair of eyes look at it, perhaps someone who works in your desired field. They will most likely have some valuable insight to share with you. Your resume will adjust over time. Before you send it off to apply for a job, be sure you're happy with it and know that it will get you in the door for the interview. Does it accurately reflect your personal brand? Be sure it reflects who you are and where you are going in your career. Just a reminder, make sure a few key words from the job description and what they're looking for are included as well, for those word generators. You want your application to be noticed.

It's a good idea to always keep your resume up to date, as you accomplish new things, so it is sort of a work in progress.

YOUR ONLINE PRESENCE

Another piece to your professional branding and portfolio is your online presence. Your online presence is more important than ever nowadays. Even if you're a private person and prefer to remain anonymous online, potential employers will look for you online and most likely find you. It's much better to have control of how you're represented in the interwebs. There are many avenues and tools to help you. You've heard of all the popular social media outlets—LinkedIn, Facebook, Instagram, TikTok, and X. The list will go on. Even a quick Google search can help someone find you. Companies and organizations looking to hire new talent will want to make sure their future staff members are not affiliated with any inappropriate content online. Just like many companies looking into one's criminal record if applicable, the same goes for your reputation as an employee and as a person in general. Your online presence is your voice.

Your Online Bio:

Your online bio can be simple and brief, but it is very important. You will be using it for your LinkedIn profile, an online job application, or on a professional site at some point. Keep it up to date and keep it handy. No one likes to read anything boring, so spice it up a bit to show your uniqueness. Give one piece of personal information that stands out about you. Maybe you have a special skill or interesting hobby. Choose one to share and open with to hook your audience.

Next, make a brief statement about what you do for work and who you are.

Then list your education and training. Again, brief and concise gets read more often.

Make it interesting. What makes you stand out from the rest? Like your resume, your bio will also be a work in progress because your focus may change over time as your career evolves. Think of it as a live and active piece, just like your resume. Keep these updated always. I will share my LinkedIn bio with you here:

> *"A California native, I naturally embrace the outdoors! I enjoy hiking and biking by the beach, but my greatest passion is helping people succeed! I am a nationally certified career counselor who helps people start a new*

*career and build their success skills by creating a career
plan that aligns with who they truly are."*

Here you can see there is something personal to start with, a key value/mission, my profession and what I do. Notice this is very brief and to the point.

More on Your LinkedIn Profile:

When you've created a unique bio, you can focus on the other pieces of your LinkedIn profile. This is where recruiters and hiring managers will search for you. A lot of times, what you show here is the first glimpse they have of who you are. They are looking to learn more about you. You'll want to make a good first impression.

Input the bio you've just written into your LinkedIn profile at the top. Below this, you'll input your past work and internship experience (like your resume). I would recommend listing your accomplishments here, more than your job duties and tasks—whereas in your resume you listed both. On your online profile, just highlight what you accomplished in each job. This may be something like "exceeding company goals." Note that subjective statements don't have the same impact as listing something more objective. For example, how did you exceed company goals? By how much? Give concrete information.

At the bottom you'll notice an option to input your education and any certifications you've earned. Also, you can select skills you have that pertain to your field. Your LinkedIn contacts will be able to endorse your skills on your profile over time as you demonstrate those skills at some point. This is also why it's good to build your network on LinkedIn. Your current and past colleagues can help attest to the skills you've listed on your profile.

Another handy feature is having professional recommendations directly on your LinkedIn profile for others to see. When it is an appropriate time, you can request that a colleague or supervisor write a brief recommendation for you. You get to see it and decide if you want to publish it on your profile or not. Just remember, you would save this option for only those you've worked with and who will have positive things to share about you.

You'll also notice options to connect to different professional organizations on LinkedIn and to follow leaders in your field.

Make your profile your own and make it work for you. You'll not only be using it to represent yourself to recruiters but also to connect to the grander network of professionals in your field. It is a free tool at your fingertips.

Be sure to use a professional-looking photo as your profile picture. You will be communicating with recruiters and employers looking to hire, as well as other professionals. Your language and messaging should be professional and kind. Always show gratitude to those helping you and reaching out to you.

More Online Tips:

If you are on other social media sites, keep them professional as well, including an appropriate photo of yourself and discreet content, etcetera. This will all reflect on you and is part of your personal branding. Be smart about which groups you follow and engage with. The internet is not as private as we think it is, even when we use privacy settings.

PERSONAL AND PROFESSIONAL REFERENCES

The next piece of your professional portfolio and personal branding is your list of references, those who can vouch for you. You will need the following:

- A list of professional references with their contact information (three to five)
- Letters of recommendation (minimum two)

These two items above will make your portfolio much stronger. Ask a colleague, a leader, or instructor/trainer—who can speak to your work ethic, personality, creativity, and talent—to be a professional reference. Sometimes job applications will ask for personal references too. This is when you can use friends and peers. But if they are asking for professional references only, really be selective about who you ask. Ask someone you know who will say positive things about you. Perhaps one or more of these will also write you a letter of recommendation for a particular job you really want. It will be impressive if you volunteer to provide a letter to your potential employer where someone is raving about you.

When applying for a job and going to an interview, have your list of references and letters of recommendation handy. These are part of your professional portfolio to present if allowed (some companies and organizations will not allow this). You can ask ahead of time or even at the end of an interview and have them ready to go.

I do want to stress how important it is to choose the right references. I've had people ask me to be a reference, but we hadn't spoken in many years. It was awkward trying to figure out what to share about them. One person who I barely knew asked me for a letter of recommendation. Needless to say, I didn't know what to put in the letter! You don't want to be embarrassed when the hiring manager speaks to your reference or reads the letter of recommendation and there's not much the person can say about you. This is obvious to the person reading it and will hurt your chances of landing the job.

One time, when I was working in law school admissions, one of our applicants asked their college professor for a letter of recommendation. Well, apparently, this applicant wasn't much of a student because the letter said, "Michael so and so asked me for a letter of recommendation. This is that letter. Sincerely, Mr. Professor." And that was it. That was all the letter said. Yikes! This really hurt the applicant's chances of being admitted because it spoke volumes about that student, that his professor had nothing good to say about him.

You know the moral of the story, my friend. Be careful who you choose to be your personal and professional reference. Be sure to ask if it would be okay to use them as a reference beforehand. It's not the best situation if they're receiving a random phone call from a company claiming you said they were your reference, but they didn't know and are not prepared. This is embarrassing. One tip I have for you is to start building your network of supporters—professors, trainers, counselors, peers, and supervisors who can really share a lot about your work performance and character.

Are you ready to submit that job application and want to include a cover letter? Read the following helpful tips first.

WRITING A COVER LETTER OR LETTER OF INTEREST

Some job applications will ask for this, some won't. Be sure to provide exactly what the instructions on the application are asking for. No more or no less. A cover letter, also known as a letter of interest, should be no more than one page, just like the resume. Remember, the manager doesn't want to have to read too much. They are already reading a lot about other applicants. Be sure to date your letter and address a person, perhaps the hiring manager specifically. If you don't have a name, you can address it "To whom it may concern . . ." or "Dear hiring committee . . ." etcetera.

Have an opening statement, a middle paragraph, and an ending statement. Then sign off with gratitude and with your full name and contact information. Below are some tips for writing your letter of interest.

Opening Statement: Introduce yourself with your full name and why you are applying for the position. State the specific position here. Perhaps mention how you heard about the open position. Did someone in their company mention it to you? Did a professional in your field say you would be perfect for the role? If so, mention this.

The middle paragraph—the "meat and potatoes," as I like to call it—is where you'll tell your story of why you think this role is a good fit for you. Here, explain how you meet the minimum and desired qualifications. Reminder, these can be found in the job announcement. Be sure to check this before writing your cover letter. When you describe how you meet the job's qualifications, be sure to quantify and qualify whenever possible. But most importantly, this is your opportunity to tell your story, the deeper meaning of why you want this job.

Then you'll have an ending statement (shorter paragraph). Here you want to thank them for taking the time to read your letter and for their consideration of you for the job. Ask them to please contact you if they have any questions.

Sign off with a sincere "Thank you" or "Sincerely" or "All my best"

Then your name...

Then your phone number and email address...

Your cover letter or letter of interest will accompany your resume when you apply for the job. Most jobs nowadays are posted online, and you will be applying online, so be sure to use .pdf files for your resume and letter. This will ensure there won't be any changes to your documents due to uploading glitches, etcetera.

Just a little side note: People like to hear stories. This makes things more interesting, instead of having a ton of information thrown at us. It's nice to conceptualize information. Always be ready to tell your story. This is the story that makes you unique from other applicants and tells them who you are and how you arrived at this place in your career. Discuss how you came to care about this type of work. This is the *why* we talked about in earlier chapters. Telling your story will make you stand out and will make you more memorable in an interview. So, take the opportunity to share your personal story in your cover letter and in your interview.

YOUR JOB SEARCH

There are many job search sites that can be very helpful in connecting you with companies, agencies, and organizations. This is especially helpful when they don't post jobs on their own company website. Employers announce job openings on these sites all the time. Below is a list of some popular ones, but there are many more than this.

- Indeed.com
- LinkedIn.com
- Careerbuilder.com
- Monster.com
- Simplyhired.com
- Ziprecruiter.com
- Glassdoor.com
- Snagajob.com
- Ladders.com

If you are after a specific role in one industry, it may be helpful to find out if your industry has its own job search site. This will help narrow down the open positions to the job you are looking for. Also, some employers only post on these career-related sites, and therefore you won't find their job announcements on the general sites above. For example, EdJoin.com is an industry-related job site for educators or for jobs that are in all levels of education. Look to see if your field has a job site like this. As you search for jobs, you should be looking for openings on both job search sites and company websites (usually in the human resources section). LinkedIn is popular these days, and recruiters are actively looking for talent on this site. So, use LinkedIn to find job announcements as well. In some cases, you can even apply through the site.

When applying be sure to input accurate and honest information into your application. If you're not sure about something, find out before including it. After you have found some good prospects and submitted your job application, resume, and cover letter, see how you can prepare for a possible interview in the next section.

INTERVIEW PREP

Invited for an interview? Great! Here's how to prepare. Interviews will usually last thirty to forty-five minutes for entry-level and mid-level positions. You may be meeting with one person only or a panel of a few people. The interview is usually a formal setting but read the room. If there is space for a pleasant conversation, take the opportunity to show them your personality and who you are. Take a deep breath, relax, and know that it's okay to be human. If it's meant for you, it will happen. If it's not, something better for you will come along. However, we always want to reflect on ourselves and see how we can learn from our experiences so we can continue to get better and better with each interview.

When you are contacted to schedule an interview, be sure to ask any logistical questions then. It may be the human resources office or the actual hiring manager who is contacting you. Don't be too shy to ask any questions that will help bring you clarification before the interview. Communication through phone or email is just fine. Things to think about:

- Date and time of interview
- Location (building/suite, etcetera)
- Contact-person to ask for once you arrive
- How many people will be on the interview panel?
- Is it acceptable to bring copies of your resume/portfolio?
- Parking details

To prepare for interview questions, review the job description well long before the interview. Visit the company's website and get a feel for what they're all about. Get to know their mission and how they represent themselves. This will give you insight into what they value. Write down questions you anticipate they might ask you about. Think about how you'll answer these. Some questions will be specific to your work experience and training and how you are prepared for the role.

Review how you will discuss this. Be prepared to talk about what you are bringing to the table, your skills, knowledge, etcetera. A few more general questions may come up that are similar to the following:

- Why are you leaving your current job? Or why did you leave your last job?
- What attracted you to this company and this position?
- Where do you see your career in five years?
- What are your strengths and weaknesses?

These are general questions to get to know you and your history. The following are behavioral questions that may come up as well:

- Tell us about a time you dealt with conflict at work.
- You encounter X scenario at work. How would you handle it?
- What would be your approach to X type of project?

You may not have any idea what the interview questions will be, but practicing the types of questions above can help prepare your mind for what comes up during an interview. Again, think about how you would answer these questions. Brainstorming your answers will also help you answer other questions you weren't anticipating because you will have put a lot of thought into it beforehand. Think about your story and what brought you to this place in your career. Again, people always love to hear meaningful and sincere stories. Keep it brief. But do share the human side of you. Make note, ahead of time, of all the things you want to share in the interview that are significant and important for the hiring manager to know in terms of why you are the best candidate for the job. Writing this down will help you remember it later.

I will share with you tips on how to answer these general interview questions and behavioral questions later in this chapter, if you would like to consider some ideas and strategies.

Day of the interview: Be sure to leave home early and arrive at the interview location early in case there's any traffic, setbacks, or trouble finding parking, etcetera. Give yourself plenty of time and breathing room so you are not stressed before the interview. You want to set yourself up to do your best.

During the interview, be sure to use professional language that is appropriate. Now is not the time for familiar talk, even if you know someone on the panel. Toward the end of an interview, when they ask you if you have anything else you would like to share, ask permission to distribute the following information (resume, references, letters of recommendation). If they say yes, then go ahead and hand out your information, especially if the interview is going well, and you feel the company is a good fit for you. You'll feel the vibe. This is also a good time to share your personal story, if you haven't already. It can be heartfelt or funny. Just show them your human side.

The interview is for the company to get to know you and see if you're a good fit for their work culture, but it's also for you to get to know them to make sure it's a good fit for you. So be sure to ask any of your burning questions. This shows your level of interest and initiative as well.

Ideas for questions are

- any questions you might have about the job description for clarification…
- What are the expectations of this role in terms of numbers and quotas, if any?
- How would you describe the work culture at this company?
- Why is this position available?
- What is the main goal of this role in the next year?

Get the idea? You don't want to ask too many questions here but show enough interest and curiosity because you may want to know the answers before starting the position. Now is your chance to find out! Again, you're assessing the position to see if you want it as well, not just if they want you. Gauge the conversation if it calls for more questions.

Warning! Now is not the time to ask about the salary. That can be discussed later if and when you're offered the position. On rare occasions you might have someone ask if you're okay with X salary. You can answer by saying, "I'm open." If you say yes right away, you take away your power to negotiate your salary later. Keep in mind, most interviews will not discuss salary but be prepared with this diplomatic answer just in case. You can even ask "what is the pay range?" This leaves the door open, so when they do offer it, you can think about the salary you feel is fair for the amount and level of work you will be providing in the role.

Some basic notes:

- If there is more than one interviewer, make eye contact with every interviewer on the panel.
- Smile and relax
- If you're nervous, take deep breaths. This will calm you.
- Sit up straight, stand tall, and be confident in what you've got to offer.

Sharing Your Professional Portfolio in an Interview:

If you have previous work that you were able to create and that really shines, or if you have praise from others in writing, you can include these in your portfolio. Just be sure copies are organized neatly. Maybe you created a brochure or have a chart showing your progress in your previous job with numbers, etcetera. This can be in your portfolio that you share in the interview.

A beginner portfolio is fine, but know that you will build this over time, with more experience and training. Once you have these pieces together, you will have a solid professional portfolio to share. Remember, this represents you and your personal brand as a professional. You are marketing yourself to potential employers you're interested in working for.

In summary, your bio, resume, cover letter, job application, and portfolio of work should be consistent, and all reflect your personal brand. If you're stuck figuring out what you want your brand to be, start by brainstorming and freewriting your thoughts about who you are and what you care about. This is a good start. Once you start to see a pattern, you can highlight these throughout the above items and think about ways to reflect this identity in your resume, online bio, portfolio, etcetera.

Below is a summary shown in a diagram for the visual learners reading this book. You can see how every item is connected somehow.

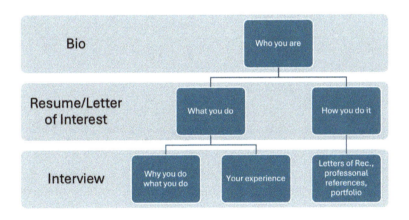

When you are prepared for a job interview, you are going to feel so confident. Below are some more in-depth ways you can prepare for interview questions.

Tips and Strategies for Answering Different Types of Interview Questions:

How to explain how you are prepared for the job and why you are a good candidate . . .Discuss your background and personal story in terms of how you decided to work in this field and why you care about this particular role. Discuss how your education, training, and experience has prepared you for the role. Take your time here. A few minutes is fine. They are generally rooting for you and hope to find things about you that are a good fit. They want to find a good candidate. It makes their life easier if they do. If they don't, then they have to keep interviewing candidates, and that's a lot of work.

How to answer general interview questions (examples below) . . .

Question: Why are you leaving your current job? Or why did you leave your last job?

Answer: Be sincere here but avoid saying negative things. If it was a bad situation, turn it into a positive. For example, "My current or last job served me well for a season, as I gained a lot of experience and learned a lot, but I am looking to grow in a different direction now."

Again, this is only an example of a diplomatic answer. You should come up with one that fits your situation. Maybe there is something about this potential company that draws you more than your current or last job did. This type of response is honest but doesn't reflect badly on anyone—yourself or your current or previous employer. If an interviewee talks badly about their old manager or employer, it reflects badly on the interviewee more than anything else. My sister and I always say, "How a person does one thing is how they will do everything else." So, this new employer wouldn't want you bad-mouthing them later, after you've worked for them. Show class and integrity here. I know you will. It's just a reminder.

Question: What attracted you to this company and this position?
Answer: Here you want to share your professional focus and how it aligns with their company or organization's mission. Discuss why you feel this position is a good fit for you.

Question: Where do you see your career going in five years?
Answer: You can talk about your career goals here. Think about the skills you want to further develop, what you see yourself doing in this role, and where you grow from there. This shows ambition and willingness to work hard. They will appreciate your enthusiasm.

Question: What are your strengths and weaknesses?
Answer: Just like the first question, you don't want to say anything negative about yourself. Discuss your strengths that pertain to the job and then explain how you have grown in a particular area and hope to continue to grow in this area. This way you're being honest but positive about how you see both your strengths and your areas of improvement.

I don't like to view these as trick questions they're throwing at you. I don't presume they want to trick you. But your answers can be very revealing of the truth, so they are just looking to get to know you and see if you will work well on their team. It's a good thing. I have found it helpful to show a willingness to learn as well.

How to answer behavioral questions (examples below)

Question: Tell us about a time you dealt with conflict at work.
Answer: Here you want to strategize. Have you heard of the CAR method (Hemming 2016)? Discuss the details of the challenge or conflict, then what your actions were to resolve it. And finally, what were the results of your actions?

Challenge—What happened?

Action—How did you handle it?

Results—What happened as a result of your actions?

This is a nice brief way to share the story and get your point across. Maybe they don't ask about a conflict but any type of situation. Try the STAR method (Gage 2022), which is similar to CAR:

Question: You are given a work scenario, and they ask you how you would handle it. Or they ask you to share a similar scenario you might have had at your past jobs.
Answer:

> **Situation:** Describe the situation (deadlines, work environment, protocol, etcetera)
>
> **Task:** Describe your task/responsibility.
>
> **Action:** What action did you take?
>
> **Results:** What did you accomplish?

Question: They can also ask you what your approach would be with a certain type of project. Here, they want to see how you think on your feet and how your skills will apply to a certain situation.
Answer: Use this question as an opportunity to show how your experience will kick in. Demonstrate how your knowledge and skills will be of value for the project.

All in all, be sure you take your time in answering questions with careful thought and consideration. The interview is your opportunity to expound on your expertise, to learn more about the position, and to shine. No need to rush through it. Practicing how you will answer interview questions will help you do much better.

"Believe you can and you're halfway there" (Krull, 2019).

—Theodore Roosevelt, 26th president of the United States (1901 to 1909)

ACCEPTING A JOB OFFER

Accepting a job offer is exciting! After a job interview that goes well, write down some of your thoughts about the position. Maybe you thought of additional questions you didn't get to ask in the interview. If you receive a phone call or email with an offer, now is the time to discuss any questions or concerns you may have, or any additional information with the hiring manager prior to accepting the offer. They will usually let you know what the pay is at the time of the offer. If you are expecting something different, it's okay to give it some thought before accepting right away. Perhaps you are expecting higher pay, or the role sounds different now. You're not hurting your chances by giving yourself some time to think about the offer and decide whether it is good for you or not. If you're unsure at the time of the offer, let them know you will need to get back to them. Below is an example:

> *"Thank you so much for the offer! I am excited about this opportunity and really enjoyed meeting everyone. Can I give it some thought and get back to you by <u>X</u> date?"*

If you decide to accept the position, wonderful. Let them know in a timely manner. If you decide you would like to ask for more pay or other adjustments, be prepared. Research what the median pay is for the position and what level of knowledge and experience would put you at the top of the pay range for this position. Be realistic in terms of your level of experience and where it falls within the pay range. Have a number or range in mind, in case they ask you what pay you were hoping for. This should be fair for both parties. Contact the person who offered you the job in a timely manner. Below is a formula that has worked for me when negotiating my salary or asking for a promotion or raise:

- Express gratitude and appreciation.
- Discuss the information you found in your research (median pay, etcetera.).

- Discuss what you're bringing to the table. Here you may need to reiterate what was discussed in the interview (your value based on the experience and knowledge you bring).
- Explain how you were expecting more pay to suit your financial needs and if there is anything they can do to increase it.

Don't go into too much detail in this conversation. Remember, concise and to the point is much more effective. Share important and relevant information and again, always show gratitude and humility. There's nothing worse than someone who is arrogant and demanding. Eek! We must check our ego at the door. If they come back and say they can't offer you more money, then you can decide if you still want the position. If you do, you can still negotiate a consideration for higher pay later, after you have proven yourself. For example, I accepted a position years ago on one condition: They agreed to consider a promotion after I worked there for at least six months, based on my performance. This promotion led to higher pay and a better title in due time. You must decide what is valuable to you at that time. Is it gaining experience? Is it higher pay? Or is it just getting your foot in the door to make yourself known? Weigh your options to figure out what is vital to your career at this time. It may be having enough money to pay your bills, or it may be just getting the opportunity to work in the field you desire. The point is to get as much as you can out of this opportunity based on your current needs at the time.

This chapter covers a lot of information about branding yourself and successfully building the pieces to market yourself and land the job you want and need in this time. Whether you are volunteering, interning, or working part-time or full-time, there is always room for improvement and sharpening of your skills so you can thrive and succeed toward your long-term career and life goals. In the next chapter you'll find helpful tips and strategies for success that you can immediately apply in your life.

"Branding is what people say about you when you are not in the room" (Allan, 2023).

—Jeff Bezos, businessman, media proprietor, and investor

Journal Prompt: Write down a description of what you want your personal brand to be. Be specific.

CHAPTER 7

Succeed by Focusing on Your Personal and Professional Skills

Ever notice how amazing some people can be at what they choose to do? For example, when you hear a great public speaker like Tony Robbins, or you see someone who excels at their talent so much, like Taylor Swift. You're just in awe and wonder how they got to this place. Well, let's be honest, it takes hard work, perseverance, and well, confidence. They believed in themselves, no matter their failures and setbacks along the way. I tell people, jump right in, and be prepared to make mistakes! Failures are the steppingstones to success. It is helpful if you have a growth mindset, rather than a fixed mindset. A growth mindset reminds us that we can grow by having learning experiences. I used to be really hard on myself and wanted to be perfect at what I did. This caused a lot of unnecessary stress and disappointment, not to mention an unrealistic standard that I could never reach. I realized that I could learn from my mistakes and get better. No one is perfect.

Everyone has their own learning journey as well. I've noticed a common theme when meeting with students and clients who are going through hard times. They often feel defeated. They express how their circumstances keep them from reaching their goals. I can see in their eyes they feel that things will never get better. I remind them that things will not always be the same. Personal circumstances and hardships change over time. We all go through different seasons, and some are tougher than others. It's how we handle them that makes a difference. So, it matters how you see yourself and how you see your situation. You and your current life season will evolve over time. Be patient and keep your eye on the prize—your goal.

BUILDING CONFIDENCE

I once met with a client who was having a difficult time accepting that she was capable and worthy of the job she really wanted. After discussing the possibilities and why she should go for that job, we discovered that she felt as though she wouldn't be good enough. She was intimidated by the possibilities. She had a fear of failure, it turns out. She would rather go after something that was easier for her to achieve. This is very common. Everyone goes through it at some point. But we must not sell ourselves short because we're afraid of making a mistake. We will make mistakes. That's a fact of life. We're only human. The good news is that mistakes will help us learn to be better. It's a journey. Some people will experience this fear a little more strongly, and it's often referred to as imposture syndrome. This is the fear that you don't belong, and that someone will find out at some point, and you will be exposed. That's a stressful feeling. If you experience this, remind yourself that everyone must start at the beginning and learn. No one is born knowing exactly what to do. It might help to work on building your confidence. Revisit that list of things you do well and what your friends and family say you're good at, discussed in Chapter 5.

Let's discuss how to build your confidence, with specific exercises. If you are prepared, you will feel more confident about your abilities and be better prepared for projects and meetings.

When it comes to self-confidence, your self-perception is vital. Do you believe in your abilities? Do you believe you can work hard at something and achieve it? Do you know that even though you make mistakes, you are good at what you do? Know your strengths. Did you know that your natural strengths are developed and usually fixed by age fifteen? You can still learn new skills later, but being aware of your natural strengths will help you choose the right career and will help you in the workplace as you tackle your tasks and duties. Know your skills and what comes naturally to you. Use your skills. If you're not sure what they are, ask family and friends who know you the best. There are strengths and skills assessments you could take that can help guide you (discussed in chapter 5). Free online assessments are included in the reader's resources section at the back of this book.

I remember when I was younger, I was confident in my abilities, but I would still get so nervous in job interviews that I would not be able to think. My mind would go blank. My anxiety and panic would debilitate me. Needless to say, it made it difficult for me to land a job. Unfortunately, the interviewers didn't get a chance to see my talent and potential, or that I had such a great work ethic. I became so discouraged that I just wanted to give up. What I found was that I needed to connect my confidence in my job skills to the confidence in my interview skills. Now when I meet with clients going through a similar situation, I can deeply relate and feel their pain. I help them to come up with a plan for how they can gain confidence and truly believe they are qualified for the job they are applying for.

I have a few strategies to share with you that I found very helpful. Ask yourself the following:

- What are my natural strengths?
- What are some skills I've acquired with my life experiences?

Write down your answers. Now, think of ways you can sharpen those skills and further develop them. Write these ideas down too. Everyone is unique and has gifts to offer the world. If you know what yours is already, great. If you don't, that's fine too. You will discover your talents. Next, use your list of strengths to write down "I am" statements. Below are some examples.

- I am confident.
- I excel at my work.
- I am kind.
- I have good people skills.
- I am talented.

Take a few minutes now to do it. You'll have a list of "I am" statements when you're done, like the ones above.

It's normal to have self-doubt from time to time. Everyone goes through it. We question our ability to do something or might feel we're just not good enough. Hey, we're only human. We're allowed to make mistakes, right? When you challenge yourself and try something new, making mistakes means you're trying and you're growing. What do we do with mistakes? We learn from them and say, "I won't do that again!" or "I'll take a different approach next time." How will we know how we want to grow and become our best if we don't learn what not to do? You've heard the saying "Without failures there is no success." It's so true.

Now create and recite a unique mantra that is just for you. Take the list of your "I am" statements that you wrote and add some additional "I am" statements with strengths that you would like to improve in yourself. You might have already included these. Maybe you have a career in mind for your future and realize there is a missing skill you need to learn. You will learn it! Put it down. Then circle each strength that you feel you need to further develop but truly desire to gain. Now, write an affirmation statement and only include those strengths you circled. It can be one or two sentences. Short enough that eventually you'll remember it. Once you have created a statement that makes you feel good about your ability to improve those skills, write it down somewhere you will be able to see often. This is your daily mantra. Read this out loud every morning before you begin your day. It will be a reminder of who you are and who you believe you can become. If we desire something, we already have a piece of it in ourselves. We just need to believe in it and take action to develop it.

I'm going to share something personal about myself. Below is my own mantra (affirmation statement), just to give you an idea as you write your own:

> *"I am worthy of success in all areas of my life, including personal relationships and in work. I help people to live in their full potential."*

Now, write yours. Take enough time to give it some good thought and fine-tune it.

Your daily affirmation/mantra, if you're consistent, will help you build your confidence. Did you fine-tune your mantra yet?

Write your mantra here:

_____

_____

_____

Take a deep breath and breathe in confidence. Don't be afraid to make mistakes. When I first start anything new, it can feel scary, or I may feel unsure of my ability to do it. Sometimes we just need a little practice before getting the hang of it. There is nothing wrong with that. No matter how talented someone is, they must start somewhere: at the beginning. Believe in your ability to learn something new and to practice and become good at it. We tend to do well when we're doing something we enjoy and get to use our skills in doing so. This is good to keep in mind when choosing an area of study or a career. Look for something that will allow you to use your natural strengths and learned skills. Confidence will come a lot easier for you.

"I've failed over and over and over again in my life. And that is why I succeed" (Febrian, 2024).

—Michael Jordan, businessman and former professional basketball player

Journal Prompt: What do I feel like and look like when I am confident? When I am confident, I feel_____.
When I am confident, I look like _____.

Visualize what you just wrote. In your mind's eye, picture what you look like when you are the most confident, when you are successful. Picture how you feel when you are in this confident state. This visualization makes it more real and tangible.

Another good exercise that builds confidence is standing up and taking up space with your body (arms, legs, etcetera). Open up your arms high and wide. Stand wide and straight. This big body movement tricks the mind into feeling confident. Our body and mind are so interconnected that this simple trick can be very powerful. Try this before a big job interview or right before a presentation you're giving to a group of people to get that extra confidence to shine.

The three exercises I've shared with you touch on your mind, body, and soul—reciting your mantra daily (soul), visualizing your confidence (mind), and physically taking up a lot of space (body) will help you build a positive self-perception. Note that the practice of communicating your mantra to yourself daily not only reminds you of the strengths you're building but will also improve how you will communicate your strengths to others. Which brings me to the next topic: building communication skills.

COMMUNICATION SKILLS

Verbal communication is not the only type of communication. There is also body language, tone, facial expressions, active listening, and how we present ourselves to others in general. All of these say a lot about who we think we are and how we want others to see us. Hence, how you communicate is part of your personal branding. How do you introduce yourself to someone? How do you communicate what you do or want to do for work? How do you communicate a message, whether it be in person, on the phone, via email, or virtually? These are all good questions to ponder. Just like you were focusing on your strengths and abilities earlier in this chapter, likewise, being aware of how you communicate is also building your own self-awareness. Self-awareness is key to success.

Once you're aware of your communication style, you can begin to adjust and be more intentional about how to present yourself and how you make others feel, too. Maya Angelou was right when she said, "People will forget what you said, people will forget what you did, but people will never forget how you made them feel" (Angelou, 2014). This is very powerful. How do you want people to feel when they interact with you, especially when you're in a job interview or building your professional network of people? Do you want them to feel confident about your competence? Then be confident in yourself and express that in all the different types of communication, verbal or otherwise. Do you want people to feel they can approach you for help or for questions about work? Do you want people to want to help you succeed because you helped them at some point? Do you want your employer to trust that you will give good service to customers because your boss knows that your language is always composed and professional?

Remember: *How someone does one thing is how they do everything.* Generally speaking, of course. Another way to put this is how someone treats one person is how they will treat others. How you communicate something is how you will communicate it to customers or clients as well. So, find your own voice and be intentional about how you present yourself and how you interact with other professionals in your field.

Tips you might have heard from elders in your family that actually work and go a long way:

- Make eye contact with everyone you're talking to.
- Give a firm handshake when meeting others.
- Smile and be positive. People like to be around positivity.
- Enunciate and speak clearly.
- Have confident body language (standing/sitting up straight, leaning in to show you are genuinely listening to the person you're talking to).
- Show that you are comfortable being yourself, that you are comfortable in your own skin. Don't be afraid to show your personality. That's how people remember you best.
- Show gratitude and use words like "please" and "thank you."

If you ever feel nervous, stop what you're doing and take a deep breath through your nose and exhale through your mouth. Do this a few times to calm your body.

A side note for those who struggle with anxiety: If you are ever in a panic, take a deep breath through your nose and hold your breath for a bit. When you're done holding your breath, exhale through your nose. You can even count to ten while holding your breath. Then breathe out slowly. You'll notice an instant calm over your body right after you do this exercise. This cuts the panic right away.

Please use any other techniques that work for you. If you ever experience severe anxiety and/or panic attacks, please seek help from a therapist or doctor.

How else do we use communication skills? You might find yourself in a meeting, wanting to communicate your ideas or present information about a product or a plan to a team of people, or you might be emailing important steps on how to complete a task to a coworker.

You can imagine all the different ways you'll need to communicate while on the job. I remember working with a manager for one year who was very meticulous about how things were done. Johanna would follow up on each project I was working on. I often found myself unprepared for her questions. I felt she would put me on the spot at any given moment. So, I adjusted to her management style and started giving her the information before she could ask for it. This little strategy worked out great. I never again found myself in those moments of scrambling, trying to find answers. This is when I learned that I should communicate my progress in a timely manner so everyone on the team, and my manager, knew where my work stood, and there was no guessing or worrying that it wouldn't be done right.

Below are some additional communication tips:

- Keep your emails brief and to the point but use a kind tone.
- Both verbal and written communication should be clear, not leaving room for misinterpretation.
- Offer to answer any questions.
- Communicate your progress to your manager/team. Open communication is helpful for everyone.
- Ask questions when you need clarity.
- Be yourself. Just always keep in mind topics of conversation should not be too personal or inappropriate. Again, what do you want people to remember about you? How do you want them to feel around you?
- Always think before you speak.
- Be present and in the moment for any conversation. People will appreciate your attention to important matters.

The tips and strategies in this chapter will become second nature to you with a little consistent practice. Now, what happens when there is conflict? Having experienced working in many different environments over the years, I've learned not to take anything too personally. Rudeness is usually due to people having a bad day or going through a personal hardship no one knows about. Negative things going on in someone's life can cause them to act indifferent and more irritable than usual. Most of the time they don't realize how they're making others feel. I know I've had my share of bad days, where I'm just not myself. You will too. It's okay. We're all only human. Cut yourself some slack, and others too. If you're being treated badly by a coworker, a supervisor, customer, or whoever, it's also okay to acknowledge it, especially if it's ongoing. It's not okay if it continues. We must have our boundaries. In general, a difference of opinions among team members is healthy, not necessarily a bad thing. People can grow from this. Practice your active listening skills and be open.

> "The biggest communication problem is that we don't listen to understand. We listen to reply" (Joseph, 2023).
>
> —Stephen R. Covey, educator, author, businessman, and speaker

This brings me to the next topic: Conflict resolution.

CONFLICT RESOLUTION

I try to check my emotions at the door whenever I remember to and try not to take anything too personally. When you encounter a disagreement or mistreatment or any challenging incident at work, the best thing to do is to stop and breathe. Observe the situation, the person, and yourself. How is this making you feel right now in the moment? Try not to react emotionally; in your mind, just acknowledge how it's making you feel. We often say things we regret because we didn't stop to think first. We just react out of pure emotion because we are frustrated or insulted or feel disrespected or unheard. It's understandable, and it's okay. That's why I said stop and observe how you feel. It helps to acknowledge it in your mind and accept that it's okay you feel this way. It slows things down so you can think before you speak.

It's also known as "the pause." You stay in control of your emotions and behavior, even if the other person talking to you is out of control. At least you're the one who stays professional and composed in the situation. Oftentimes, it's just human reaction without thinking; less often is it personal. Don't allow someone else's poor attitude to affect you too much. Let's stay positive and keep your mind thinking clearly so you are the one working well under pressure, and you are the one coming up with clear and effective solutions. Trust me, team members and your supervisor will greatly appreciate your ability to remain calm and not take anything too personally.

Now, if bad treatment is ongoing, day after day, you will need to speak up and stand up for yourself while remaining calm and composed. You respect yourself enough to let your boundaries be known to others. You will need to address it and acknowledge the bad behavior with the person. Again, check your emotions at the door. Don't bring it up when you're still upset about the incident or when the other party is still upset. Maybe even sleep on it first. Then, when you bring it to the person's attention, you are calm and unemotional about it. Don't accuse the person of anything, just state the facts of what happened.

Exchange 1

You: "Yesterday I noticed you snapped at me when I told you how I was working on X project."
Other Person: "What are you talking about?! I didn't snap at you! You're being too sensitive."

Exchange 2

You: "After our conversation about the project yesterday, I felt uneasy. Is everything okay with you?"
Other Person: "What do you mean? About the project? Well, I think it should go this way . . ."

In Exchange 1, the person is defensive right off the bat and turns it around to make it seem like you're doing something wrong. They don't own their part of it.

In Exchange 2, it's more about how you felt after the conversation with them, not what they did wrong. But you're still acknowledging something they did to make you feel uncomfortable. This makes them more aware of it, and hopefully next time they'll pause and think twice before speaking. It helps to indirectly acknowledge bad behavior in a non-accusatory manner. Note, this is not being passive aggressive. This is acknowledging the elephant in the room without putting the other person on the defense. You want to maintain a peaceful and healthy work environment for yourself.

If this method doesn't work, and they continue to react based on their stressed state, you may need to bring in a third party to help mediate. If your job entails working closely with others, you will learn to work with different personalities and different attitudes. Try not to let any of it affect you. Just try to create positive energy. Someone has got to do it, right? Also, you want to keep your mind clear and calm so you can focus on doing a good job at work. This is your career you're building, and no one will take care of it as much as you will.

In this life we play many different roles. Roles such as friend, spouse, parent, child, student, worker, mentor/mentee, etcetera. When we are in the work setting, we must stay in our work role. Be ourselves but remain in the role we were hired to do. That means staying professional. Professional in language, attitude, service, work, etcetera. People will see your work ethic and trust you to handle situations, whether positive or negative, in a professional manner. Your supervisor will trust you to represent the organization well because your behavior aligns with who they are, what their mission is. Get it? This is also important as you build rapport with your leaders and other colleagues. This is part of building your professional brand and network for any future opportunities. You want to build a positive and trusting reputation for yourself in your field.

"Peace is not the absence of conflict but the ability to cope with it" (Maharajan, 2010).

—Mahatma Gandhi, lawyer, anti-colonial nationalist, and political ethicist

TEAMWORK

What I've learned is that whether I find myself in the leader role or the team member role, it's good to have an open mind. When I was younger, I had to work on not being too shy to contribute my ideas. It's also important to be open to hearing other ideas from team members. Creating a safe space to brainstorm together really allows for more creativity and growth for all members of a team. Another thing I learned is that once the tasks are assigned to each member, trust others to get their part done well. Just as you will get your part done well too. If someone slacks off and is not meeting expectations, use your conflict resolution skills, discussed earlier in this chapter, to resolve it with the person.

Example

You: "Are you having any challenges with your part of the project? Is there anything I can do to help? Let's get you the tools you need to get it done."

All you can do is try to make things better. Remember, you never know what people are going through in their personal lives. Offer support and clarity if you can. Encourage others to do a good job. I've always believed in the importance of showing appreciation for each other's contributions, no matter how big or small. This aids in creating a supportive work environment that fosters growth, good morale, and motivation. There is always something to be grateful for.

> "It is literally true that you can succeed best and quickest by helping others to succeed" (Hill, 2008).
> —Napoleon Hill, self-help author

PRESENTING IDEAS

Hopefully we get many opportunities to present our ideas, whether it be in a staff meeting or on a call or in other ways, depending on our work environment. As mentioned, when I was young and had just started working, I was too shy and didn't know if my ideas were good enough, so I just refrained from contributing and remained quiet. What I learned was that no matter what role you're in, what level you're at, you always have the ability and uniqueness to contribute your ideas, just like anybody else.

Note that if it is a high-stakes job, the boss will look to hire people who have a strength that is missing from their team. They will delegate a task to someone who they know has a strength or talent to do it well. A smart manager will surround themselves with people who do certain things better than they can. This creates a team with a diverse set of talents that will not only get the job done but will also make that manager look good by doing it well. If you make your boss look good, they'll most likely want to keep you around for the long term. My mentor used to tell me, "If your boss loves you, that is job security."

So, go ahead! Be you and show off your uniqueness. That's why you were hired, my friend. Just understand that not all your ideas will be accepted, and that's okay. At least you're showing effort and enthusiasm for your work. If you care about the cause, the goal, the work, others will too. You will also inspire others to do a good job. Use the communication skills we talked about earlier to present your ideas. Be positive and open to tweaks and other opinions regarding your ideas.

It's best to have your ideas well thought out before offering them to others. It helps to first take notes of your ideas. Look at each idea from all angles and different scenarios. How will your idea help? Keep in mind the goal. Does it help the goal? Does it offer a solution? If so, how? How will you measure the effectiveness and results of your idea? Be ready for questions from others. People like to work with solution-based team members, rather than those who complain but offer no problem-solving ideas. Another thing I used to think was that people want the status quo, because that's what they're used to. They avoid change because they want to remain comfortable. Although this may be true for some, life is in a constant state of change. We should all embrace that fact and not be afraid of change and the evolution of the way things are, the status quo. Sometimes we get scared of the unknown or simply scared of not knowing what to expect. It's okay. Remember, acknowledge your fears and uncertainty but then let go of them; let them pass. Stay positive, and you will attract more positivity at work and in your life. Our attitude and mindset make a difference. The energy you put out there is exactly what you will attract back into your life.

More tips on presenting ideas:

Use visual aids. These can be charts, pictures, tables, physical demos, etcetera.

Use the "sandwich" method. Discuss the bread first (positive), followed by what's inside the sandwich (issue and your idea of how to solve it), and end with the bread (positive).

Example

You: "Good morning, everyone. I wanted to discuss *project X*. I know we've all been working hard on it, and we've had some hiccups, but I've really appreciated everyone's efforts. Your time and attention go a long way and make a difference in our productivity *(bread)*.

"I wanted to throw out an idea of how we can work more efficiently. What do you think if we do *B* instead of *A*? We can try it and see in two weeks how it works out. We can always tweak it and improve it if needed *(meat, cheese, tomato, etcetera)*.

"I'm grateful for this team and all you do. I'm open to any ideas. Let's discuss *(bread)*."

In the beginning, acknowledge their hard work. In the middle, present the issue and solution. In the end, show appreciation for the team's hard work and your openness to their ideas.

Humor is always nice and lightens things up and can make work more fun. Always be sure to be clear and concise. Ask if anyone needs clarification or has questions. Allow space to discuss. In fact, welcome it. My old boss used to make us laugh in our staff meetings. That really lightened up some stressful situations. Remember, your ideas are needed and welcomed in the workplace.

> "If you don't put your ideas into the world, no one else can benefit from them" (Grant, 2022).
>
> —Adam Grant, science author and professor in organizational psychology

ASKING FOR A RAISE AND/OR PROMOTION

Do you want to know how to ask for a promotion and/or pay raise at work? Whether you're hoping for one in your current job or just want to be prepared for a future opportunity, the steps below are helpful for presenting your boss with a request for a raise or promotion. Note that I would not ask for a promotion or raise unless I felt I deserved it. If you have worked hard and proven yourself, then you'll know if it's a good time to move forward.

- Express gratitude and enthusiasm for your work.
- Discuss your accomplishments since you've been working in your current role. Include what you have contributed to the team and overall goals. Perhaps you completed a training or certificate program that made you more knowledgeable in your field. Talk about what you learned. If you have received praise from others, share this. If you have done things that are above and beyond your job duties, share this too.
- Express how you would like to continue working for this organization and hope to grow your career in this organization or company.
- Request the promotion title you want and/or pay that you want. If it is not clear what the next step-up title is, you can always suggest one. It is also fine to keep your pay open and ask for whatever they can do to increase your salary or hourly wage.
- Reiterate how you hope you can work together to make this happen and continue to contribute good work.

The above is just an example of pieces to cover in your discussion and request. You will modify as needed for your specific situation. But hopefully it gives you a good sense of an effective conversation around this topic. It has worked for me in the past.

PROFESSIONAL CONNECTIONS AND NETWORKING

Building a rapport with not only the people you serve (customers or clients) but also leaders, coworkers, and colleagues is important. As mentioned earlier, this is part of your professional branding, your reputation in your field. Congruency is key.

According to the *Oxford Dictionary*, "congruent" (adjective) is defined as "In agreement or harmony." The *Cambridge Dictionary* describes it as "similar to or in agreement with something, so that the two things can both exist or can be combined without problems."

Your manner of being should be congruent. This means each part of you—what you say and what you do—should align with itself. This is genuine, authentic, and transparently you.

I remind myself; check your ego and your intentions at the door. Why am I here? What am I supposed to be doing? Why am I about to say this? What will this accomplish? What am I feeling that is making me do this or say this? Sometimes our intentions are in the unconscious mind and may affect our behavior. Bring what is in the unconscious to the conscious mind so you're aware of what is really going on. One way to do this is to pause and be aware of what you're feeling in that moment, as discussed earlier. Is it fear? Is it tension in your body? Is it insecurity? Are you tired or stressed? Do you feel like you need to prove yourself to others? Are you feeling unappreciated or unseen? Maybe it's more positive what you're feeling in the moment, like excited, open, confident, energetic. Be aware of either positive or negative feelings. Pause and acknowledge the feelings and thoughts in your mind. And of course, then breathe and let them go. If your intensions are always clear and honest, people will feel that about you and trust you. More importantly, you will be comfortable in your own skin and comfortable being who you truly are.

As you gain more work experience, you will meet more and more people in your field. It's good to always be kind and patient. Be helpful

116

to others. It's about being genuine and caring. Be your normal, personable self. Don't be afraid to show your personality my friend. People appreciate talking about things that matter and enjoy good, clean humor and wit. It's not necessarily about getting people to like you because not everyone will, but it's more about working well with others and trying your best to connect on a professional level. They will always remember that about you and how you made them feel. If you're helpful, people generally will return the favor when you need their support. You may encounter people who don't but keep doing it anyway.

You can also connect with people by attending professional mixers and events. Professional conferences are a good way to learn more about your work, and meet like-minded, driven individuals as well. This is another place where you will use your great communication skills as we talked about earlier in this chapter. Be sure to connect through LinkedIn and get their contact information. If someone gives you advice or helps you in some way, be sure to send a thank-you note right after the event. If you just had a great conversation and want to connect, be sure to send a message after, something like, "It was great meeting you. I hope we can cross paths again, maybe even brainstorm ideas. Take care." This simple connection will keep the channel of communication open and inviting. Build community on LinkedIn.

Whenever you get an opportunity to be a resource to someone, take it. Remember, what you put out into the universe will return to you in due time. The process of networking and making meaningful connections will help you grow and be prepared for new opportunities that will eventually come your way.

> "Connection requires vulnerability and the courage to be authentic and genuine" (Hamff, 2024).
>
> —Brené Brown, professor, researcher, author, and podcast host

LEADERSHIP

Were you the kid who told everyone how to play a game or had great ideas that people wanted to follow? Congratulations! You were probably born with natural leadership skills, but for the rest of us, it doesn't come as naturally. Perhaps you were chosen to lead a game or an assignment in school. Or maybe you gained some leadership skills by taking on certain tasks in your family growing up. Maybe you took on a leadership role at summer camp, or as an intern, or in the workplace. No matter how small and insignificant you might think this was, it was a learning experience for you. You learned leadership skills that will last a lifetime, believe it or not. If you remember I shared my early experiences in the introduction of this book. I washed cars when I was 11 years old, led a candy club and planned neighborhood productions with other kids. This was play and fun for me way back then, but I was learning and growing too, without even knowing. As time goes on, you will continue to sharpen your leadership skills. Maybe you'll choose to be in a management role at work. Whether you find yourself there or not, you will still find these skills to be useful in a lot of different situations.

What does it mean to be a good leader? I think of someone who is a visionary and inspires people to care about work and to work hard toward a goal. Perhaps it's someone who is like a mentor or a coach. Maybe it's someone who has people skills and can manage a team well. Is it someone who explains tasks clearly and holds their team accountable? Is it someone who works just as hard as their staff members do, not just delegates what people should do? Is it someone who motivates people and creates an inviting work environment, someone who acknowledges good work in another and shows appreciation? Or maybe it's a combination of all these things.

Whatever your definition of what a good leader is, ask yourself what kind of leader you want to be. If you want to get to a managerial or supervisory role at work, write down how you want to be as a leader. You can even look up ideas online and begin developing these skills. If you don't see yourself in a leadership role in the future, that's great too! There are plenty of other types of roles. However, you can still use leadership skills in life, so they are worth sharpening up a bit. There will be times when you work in a group and interact a lot with others. These skills will come in handy. You can learn from other leaders around you too. What are some of the things they do well that make them a good leader? What are some of the things they don't do as well? You can learn a lot from observing both what to do and what not to do.

I had an amazing boss who I learned so much from. I'll never forget him. We had a small team with a lot of work to do as we organized events for our students and helped students organize their own events on campus. It was a lot of curricular and co-curricular activities we were responsible for, very fast paced. We were happy to work hard because our boss made it fun. He used to make us laugh in meetings, yet he was very organized and taught us to be accurate in our work, so we would gain the trust and respect of the campus community. No matter how difficult someone could be, he would always show kindness and go out of his way to help them. He expressed his appreciation for our hard work and acknowledged us whenever we brought our strengths to the table. He was truly inspiring and a pleasure to work with. I learned so much from him in such a short period of time. You can begin to sharpen your own leadership skills with the activities you choose to do in your life.

"There are three essentials to leadership: humility, clarity and courage" (De Angelis, 2022).

—Fuchan Yuan, Chan Master

As you embark on your career journey, it is wonderful to work hard and stay focused. However, you must also allow yourself space to live. When life gets busy and hectic, how can we make sure we are maintaining a balanced life? How can we ensure we are performing at our best and also creating happiness in our lives?

WORK-LIFE BALANCE

You are not living to work, hopefully. You are working to live! It's important for us to remember not to allow our work to consume us. Sure, it's a big part of our lives, but it's not everything. It's a part of what we do and can become a part of who we are. But it's not all of who we are. It is just one role we play, out of many roles in our life, as discussed in Chapter 5. A healthy balanced life allows us to live in all our roles, not just our work role. Think about all your roles. Write them down on a piece of blank paper. After you have given this some thought and taken a few minutes to write them down, circle each one, but the size of each circle should reflect how big you want this role to be in your life. So, you'll have small, medium, and large circles, depending on what you desire for each role. Keep in mind, life brings on new experiences over time, and you may need to add or take away some roles later. Or your desire for a certain role may get bigger or smaller over time. It's okay if this is fluid, but for the current moment, how would you like to see your life in your current roles? Perhaps you're a college student; this is one of your roles. Maybe you're a friend, partner, leader, parent, writer, or builder. The bigger the circle you draw around a role, the more time you want to invest in that role. It's okay to have smaller roles. Keep the diagram you just drew in mind as you allot your time between roles and as you think about what type of work you want to do. Will this job or career allow you to spend the amount of time and energy in these roles that are important to you?

Other things to consider when creating a balanced life are the things you do on a regular basis, your daily routine. You can start by looking at your week. At the beginning of each week, ask yourself what your weekly goals are. What do I want to accomplish this week? Schedule time in your calendar each week for these weekly goals. Below are some examples:

- Classes/training
- Work shifts
- Exercise
- Social time
- Family time/personal commitments
- Hobbies
- Relaxation
- Leisure—doing things you enjoy, for fun
- Time spent in each of your roles

Scheduling out how you want to spend your time each week is a good way to ensure you'll be creating some balance in your life (more on time management in Chapter 1). Imagine what a sixty-hour-a-week job looks like? This may be okay for some people, depending on their other life roles. It's got to work for you, though. Everyone is different. If you find that there are some things and/or certain roles taking up too much of your time and you're not able to get to the other roles, you need to adjust your life to achieve that balance. A busy schedule requires excellent time management skills. Find a way to prioritize the things you care about, or you'll be left feeling depleted. We perform at our best when we have balance. Do you want to be a good student, friend, partner, or worker? You must create balance in your life to do so.

If you would like to change anything in your life right now, take a few minutes to take some notes and write down what changes you'll make. You may have noticed by now that I have you write things down a lot; I know. But this is the first step to getting things done. When you're creating a to-do list, what is the first thing you do? You write it down or type it, depending. This psychologically makes it a priority in our brains that we need to act and get it done.

"Balance is not something you find, it's something you create" (Hoffner, 2023).

—Jana Kingsford, author

PRACTICING GRATITUDE

I'm so grateful I grew up with a mother who was independent and confident! She was a wonderful role model in my life that reassured me that I too can be independent and learn how to take care of myself. And I don't mean financially only. It's important we know how to take care of our physical and emotional health too. My mom was very strong and determined. I appreciate having this in my life growing up. What I've learned through life is that living in a constant state of gratitude makes even the tough times better. Every day I think about what I'm grateful for. This reminds me of all the good things in my life and helps me to not dwell on the not so good things. Years ago, I used to always think about what was missing in my life. Worrying about problems would keep me up at night, and I couldn't sleep. Since I learned to be more grateful, my life has changed drastically in terms of the way I feel every day. My gratitude has brought me more things to be grateful for. When I sit in each moment of the day as though it were a gift, I feel an abundance of happiness. There is an inner joy, even on bad days where everything seems to go wrong. I'm grateful for this inner joy and peace in my life. When I meditate or pray, I am sure to be thankful for the love of my family, for my friends, the work I get to do, and my good health, rather than put in my requests for more good things. It might help to start by writing in your journal. What are all the things you're grateful for in life? Try to focus on what is and not what isn't there yet. In this very moment, are you safe? Not yesterday or tomorrow, but now? Then be in this moment and be grateful for it.

When I look back at my life so far, because I've lived about half of it, I see peaks and valleys. These represent the high moments and the low moments. I am grateful for the education and training I received, the fun experiences traveling and going to concerts, the work I get to do helping others, and most of all the people I love. I am also grateful for what I learned by going through tougher times, such as switching my career and having to start at the beginning again, going through a divorce and my life completely changing, losing my grandparents and experiencing other romantic heartbreaks along the way. I remember though, even in these times there were good moments like having the courage to go after what I want even though switching careers was scary and felt like a gamble at the time. I have good memories with the people I spent a lot of time with, even though the relationship didn't last. The deep grief of losing my grandparents is there because I loved them so much. In all these incidents, I experienced the pain of loss. But this is part of the human experience. If we love and enjoy something so much, we become attached to it, so of course it will hurt when it's gone. Whenever I feel sadness or grief, it reminds me of the love inside of me that exists and that's why they are there.

I wish I could ask you, what you gathered about who I am by reading about my peaks and valleys in life? We all have them, right? We can turn the valleys into peaks, finding the positive in something negative that has happened. You can tell a lot about a person by their personal story. When you tell your own story, people will learn more about you: how you overcame, how you view the world and who you are today.

> "If you must look back, do so forgivingly. If you must look forward, do so prayerfully. However, the wisest thing you can do is be present in the present . . . gratefully" (Romanelli, 2018).
>
> —Maya Angelou, memoirist, poet, and civil rights activist

<u>Journal Prompt</u>: What do I love to do and when do I feel the most aligned with who I am?

> "Nourish what makes you feel confident, connected, contented. Opportunity will rise to meet you" (Winfrey, 2019).
>
> —Oprah Winfrey, talk show host, television producer, actress, author, and media proprietor

MOTIVATION

Multiple factors help me get motivated, but the most important one is valuing the work that I do. If you're a college student or a new professional, there will be times when you need to work hard to get where you want to be. It's so rewarding when you do though. I've heard college students say how super motivated they are at the beginning of a semester, but mid-semester they become less motivated to work hard. Maybe they feel burnt-out. I've also heard clients explain how poor management can really demotivate them at work. Experiencing this is completely normal and human. It's how we handle it that will determine how motivated we remain over time. I would suggest choosing an area of study and a job that you care about, as discussed in Chapter 5, regarding career and life planning. If you are excited about your future or current career, you are more likely to stay motivated, even when it gets tough. Everyone comes across obstacles and setbacks from time to time. No one is exempt from this, no matter how talented they are. Be strong and keep going! Try your best to work through the hurdles. You will get there. If you find yourself in a major or career that doesn't get you excited and motivated, you need to think about making some changes, my friend.

When it comes to staying motivated when feeling rejected if our ideas are not accepted or we don't get hired for a job we really wanted, know that it's normal and acceptable to feel sad and down about it. We all go through it. Trust me, I've been denied plenty of jobs in my life. But thankfully I've also been accepted for many. It's just a part of it. We learn from it, and we grow. We get better. I realized that most of those times I was denied a job, it was a blessing in disguise. There was a better opportunity right around the corner. So, when you experience rejection, reframe it in your mind as redirection. Because that's exactly what it is. The universe is redirecting you to something bigger or better for you. Trust that. And you will remain motivated on your journey.

Another way to stay motivated is to reward yourself when you accomplish something or reach a goal, no matter how big or small it is. What are some things you enjoy? Maybe it's your favorite restaurant. Maybe it's your favorite candy or fun thing to do. It can even be a purchase of something you've been wanting for a while. It can be anything you want it to be. The point is to celebrate your wins. You will start to feel that your hard work pays off. You will have something to look forward to. Motivation fuels your emotional energy, your mental energy, and your physical energy. Below are some additional ideas for you.

- Physical activity
- Fun experiences
- Meaningful friendships
- Healthy lifestyle

In Gabrielle Bernstein's book *The Universe Has Your Back*, she shares several "universal lessons" in life. I would like to share one of them with you now. It is simple but impactful. "Universal Lesson: Your presence is your power . . . Through the power of your intentions, you can reorganize your energy in an instant" (Bernstein 2018, 20). Your intentions change your reality. That's how powerful intention setting is! This can apply to many different things. But think about this. What is your intention behind the career or area of study you are pursuing? What do you intend to accomplish by making this your life's work? Write this down in your journal and ponder it for a while. Do your daily decisions align with this intention and purpose in your life? How is this path meaningful to you? Your intentions behind everything you do will create what you intend them to and will influence the outcome.

Be open to follow your heart and follow the pull of the universe's direction. My sister (with a therapist background) and I often have these deep conversations about life. We agree that we should pay attention when life pulls us in a different direction than we thought we were going in. A lot of times we need to listen to the pull and let go of the push. Things begin to flow better, and you don't find yourself fighting against the current that pushes you back. Keep your head up my friend and stay motivated.

> "The future belongs to those who believe in the beauty of their dreams" (Goal, 2019).
> —Eleanor Roosevelt, American political figure, diplomat, and activist

FINAL THOUGHTS

I want you to think about your *why*. What is your why in life? What is your why in work? What moves you to do what you do? This is the thing that is more important than the *how* or the *who* or the *where* questions. If you know your why, the others will come together. So, if you are working hard in college and/or work and experience obstacles, always go back to your why. Why am I going to school? Why am I getting this training? Why am I working here? Why do I care about this work? Your answer is the thing that will keep you motivated and want to keep going. It will push you to move forward. Don't ever forget your why. Even if the journey looks long and daunting, always lean on your purpose and mission. It will get you through tough times.

Also, think about what impact you want to have in your life and how. When you know your why, you will find the how. Write down your why in your journal now. Then think about how you will use your gifts to fulfill your why, your mission, in work and/or in your personal life.

For your final exercise, I want you to create a vision board of your goals and dreams—and don't forget your why. This can be in any artistic or crafty medium you would like. Be creative and have fun with it. A vision board will have all your dreams reflected on it. Think big and out of the box. You don't have to limit yourself. You are worth every one of them. You can even include your mantra, which we talked about earlier. Use visuals such as drawings, magazine cutouts, graphics, words, textures, quotes, any items that move you and motivate you. They should serve as a reminder of your goals and dreams in life. It might be kind of cool to create an electronic board with your own graphics and pictures if you're good at that. I'm not! Then print the electronic board in color. The purpose of creating a vision board is so you can display it somewhere you can easily see, and it is a reminder to you every day of where you are and where you are going in life. On my vision board, I have a picture of a beautiful, Spanish-style house that I'd like to call home someday. I pin inspiring quotes on my board that will motivate me every time I look at them. Creating a vision board is a creative way to design the life you want by setting an intention, and it's very powerful in making it come true, just like writing in your journal does. That's why throughout this book I've had you write a lot of things down and use a notebook or journal you can always refer to. Living your life with intention aids in manifesting your desires. Do things on purpose, my friend.

My wish is that the tips and strategies for success that I've shared with you in this book will help you at various times in your life. Be confident in your career choices and apply your talents in the workplace and in your personal life. Remember, the world needs you. The world needs your gifts. Always be open to learning and improving and helping others along the way.

> "Success is not final; failure is not fatal; it is the courage to continue that counts" (Lodice, 2019).
>
>> —Winston Churchill, British statesman, soldier, and writer, who twice served as Prime Minister of the United Kingdom

If you have questions or feedback you would like to share, please contact me at christinasandoval.com.

BIBLIOGRAPHY

and Love, Peace. Peace Is the Result of Retraining Your Mind to Process Life as It Is, Rather Than As You Think It Should Be: Lined Notebook, Journal, Planner, Sketchbooks. Simple and Elegant, Perfect and Funny Gift for Coworker, Employee, Birthdays. (120 Pages, 6 X 9). N.p.: Independently Published, 2020.

Allan, Thomas. *Branding Brilliance: Your Blueprint to Creating & Communicating an Irresistible Personal Brand.* N.p.: KFT Publishing, 2023.

Allen PhD, Lisa Van. *Your Belief Quotient: 7 Beliefs That Sabotage or Support Your Success.* United Kingdom: Balboa Press, 2013.

Angelou, Maya. *Rainbow in the Cloud: The Wisdom and Spirit of Maya Angelou.* United States: Random House Publishing Group, 2014.

Belmont, Judith. *I did then what I knew how to do. Now that I know better, I do better. Embrace Your Greatness: Fifty Ways to Build Unshakable Self-Esteem.* United Kingdom: New Harbinger Publications, 2019.

Bernstein, Gabrielle. *The Universe Has Your Back: Transform Fear to Faith.* Carlsbad, CA: Hay House LLC, 2018.

Bolton, Anna. Once You Make a Decision the Universe Conspires to Make It Happen: Inspirational Quote for Depression & Anxiety for Women Men & Teens & Self Reflection. 160 Lined Pages with Uplifting & Funny Sayings. Motivational Exercise Book/Diary Composition & Journal. N.p.: Independently Published, 2019.

Bookz, Banoc. Success Isn't Always about Greatness. It's about Consistency. Consistent Hard Work Leads to Success. Greatness Will Come: Lined Journal Notebook. N.p.: Independently Published, 2019.

Canfield, Jack. *Key to Living the Law of Attraction.* Dearfield Beach, FL: Health

Communications Inc., 2007.

Chan, Goldie. "50 Empowering Personal Brand Quotes for Your Journey." Forbes.Com. Forbes, January 3, 2024. https://doi.org/https://www.forbes.com/sites/goldiechan/2024/01/03/50-empowering-personal-branding-quotes-for-your-journey/

Collection, Finest. Setting Goals Is the First Step in Turning the Invisible into the Visible: Journal - Diary, Notebook. N.p.: Independently Published, 2020.

De Angelis, David. *The Big Book of Aphorisms and Quotes: 2,000 Author Quotes that Will Change Your Life.* N.p.: David De Angelis, 2022.

Doran, George, Arthur Miller and James Cunningham. "There's a SMART Way to

Write Management's Goals and Objectives." Management Review - AMA Forum.

Volume 70, Issue 11 (1981): 35-36.

EDITION, Simografix. If You Are Not Willing to Learn, No One Can Help You. Journal Notebook for Students, ... Scientists. Use As Diary Or Journal: 100 White Lined Pages 6x9 in Notebook | with Zig Ziglar Quote on CoverGift Idea for Students to Write In. N.p.: Independently Published, 2021.

Frankl, Viktor. *Man's Search for Meaning*. Boston, MA: Beacon Press, 2006.

Gage, Martha. *The STAR Method Explained: Proven Technique to Succeed at Interview*. United States: Amazon Digital Services LLC - Kdp, 2019.

Garcia, Hector and Francesc Miralles. *Ikigai: The Japanese Secret to a Long and Happy Life*. City of Westminster, London: Penguin Life, 2017.

Gardner, Howard. *Frames of Mind: The Theory of Multiple Intelligences*. New York, NY: Basic Books, 1983.

Giacomucci, Carol. *The ABCs of Life: Journaling Your Way to Meaning*. N.p.: Wheatmark, Inc., 2024.

Goal, Score Your. The Future Belongs to Those Who Believe in the Beauty of Their Dreams: 110 Lined Pages Motivational Notebook with Quote by Eleanor Roosevelt. N.p.: Independently Published, 2019.

Grant, Adam. X post, January 6th 2022

Harvey Mackay. Expect to make some mistakes when you try new and different approaches. Sometimes colossal failures lead to spectacular successes. AZQuotes.com, Wind and Fly LTD, 2024. https://www.azquotes.com/quote/183043, accessed July 30, 2024.

Hemming, Allison. "The C.A.R. Technique: Your Secret Interviewing Weapon." The Hired Guns. 2016. https://the-hiredguns.com/car-technique-secret-interviewing-weapon/

Hill, Napoleon. *The Law of Success*. United States: Jeremy P. Tarcher/ Penguin, 2008.

Hoffner, Josh. "Achieving a Work/Life Balance that Suits You: Prioritizing Valuable Time with Your Family." LinkedIn.Com. May 14, 2023. https://doi.org/https://www.linkedin.com/pulse/achieving-worklife-balance-suits-you-prioritizing-valuable-hoff-ner/.

Hamff, Jeremy. How to Upgrade Your Mental Operating System. LinkedIn, June 23, 2024. https://www.linkedin.com/pulse/how-upgrade-your-mental-operating-system-pt-4-jeremy-hamff-dpnle/

Joseph, Prof. Ansi Sojan. *Understanding the Self*. N.p.: Notion Press, 2023.

Journeys, Career. "Decision Checklist." (Career Journeys, Pasadena, CA) 2016.

Krull, Casida. Believe You Can and You're Halfway There - Theodore Roosevelt: Journal with 100 Dot Grid Pages and Features a Quote by Theodore Roosevelt. Size 5 X 8. N.p.: Independently Published, 2019.

LOPEZ, Carolina. It Is in Your Moments of Decision That Your Destiny Is Shaped. -Tony Robbins: Motivational Daily Planner | Motivational Gratitude Journal |Motivational Weekly Planner| 145 Pages 8. 5 X 11. N.p.: Independently Published, 2020. Anton, Barry S. "Coping with Stress." American Psychological Association President's

Column. Volume 46, No. 11. December 2015: 5. https://www.apa. org/monitor/2015/12/pc

Maharajan, M.. *Mahatma Gandhi and the New Millennium.* India: Discovery Publishing House Pvt. Limited, 2010.

Morris, Jonathan. *The Way of Serenity: Finding Peace and Happiness in the Serenity Prayer.* United States: HarperCollins, 2014.

Pauk, Walter; Owens, Ross J. Q. "Chapter 10: The Cornell System: Take Effective Notes." How to Study in College, 10 ed., 235-277. Boston, MA: Wadsworth, 2010.

Quotes That Will Change Your Life: 100 Success Words That Will Change Your Life For the Better. N.p.: Andrea Febrian, 2024.

Romanelli, David. *Life Lessons from the Oldest and Wisest: Inspiration, Wisdom, and Humor for All Generations.* United States: Skyhorse Publishing, 2018.

Sajaganesandip, Own Work, File: Multiple-intelligence.jpg, Wikimedia Commons, the free media repository. November 1, 2015, https://commons.wikimedia.org/w/index. php?curid=45235609

Sinek, Simon. "How Great Leaders Inspire Action." May 4, 2010. YouTube video, 18.34 minutes, https://www.youtube.com/ watch?v=qp0HIF3SfI4&t=10s

SportsNotebooks. It Takes Courage to Grow Up and Become Who You Really Are: E. E. Cummings - Place for Writing Thoughts. N.p.: Independently Published, 2020.

Super, Donald E. *The Psychology of Careers.* N.p.: Harper and row, 1957.

Tolle, Eckhart. *The Power of Now: A Guide to Spiritual Enlightenment.* Novato, CA: New World Library, 2004.

Wesleyan University, Ohio. "Challenge Mindset Cards." Ohio Wesleyan Career Connection 2024.

https://cdn.uconnectlabs.com/wp-content/uploads/sites/289/2024/03/Challenge-Mindset-Cards.pdf

Adapted from J.P. Michel, SparkPath, Challenge Cards (Ottawa, Canada. 2018) version 1.3 (mysparkpath.com)

Winfrey, Oprah. *The Path Made Clear: Discovering Your Life's Direction and Purpose*. United States: Flatiron Books, 2019.

RESOURCES FOR THE READER

BOOKS

The Element: How Finding Your Passion Changes Everything by Ken Robinson

Ikigai: The Japanese Secret to a Long and Happy Life by Hector Garcia and Francesc Miralles

Key to Living the Law of Attraction: A Simple Guide to Creating the Life of Your Dreams by Jack Canfield

Man's Search for Meaning by Viktor E. Frankl

The Power of Now by Eckhart Tolle

The Seven Spiritual Laws of Success: A Practical Guide to the Fulfillment of Your Dreams by Deepak Chopra

Super Attractor: Methods for Manifesting a Life Beyond Your Wildest Dreams by Gabrielle Bernstein

Think Like a Monk: Train Your Mind for Peace and Purpose Every Day

The Universe has Your Back: Transform Fear to Faith by Gabrielle Bernstein

You Are a Badass: How to Stop Doubting Your Greatness and Start Living an Awesome Life by Jen Sincero

VIDEOS—YOUTUBE

"Grit: The Power of Passion and Perseverance" TED Talk by Angela Duckworth

"How Great Leaders Inspire Action" TED Talk by Simon Sinek

WEBSITES

Bls.gov/ooh/

CareerOneStop.org

MyNextMove.org

ONetOnline.org

UC Berkeley Career Center: https://career.berkeley.edu/start-exploring/majors-to-career/what-can-i-do-with-a-major-in/